AFTER THE CALL

A FIRST RESPONDER'S GUIDE TO PTSD

Virginia Cruse
Katie Salidas

ISBN: 978-1-7348067-8-6

Published by: Military Counseling Center San Antonio, PLLC
MilitaryCounselingSA.com
www.TheSoldiersBlog.com

Edited by: Rebecca Keeler

Interior Layout and Cover Design by: Rising Sign Books
RisingSignBooks.com
KatieSalidas.com

Since 2022, it has been my greatest honor to work with inspiring leaders who are dedicated to community mental health and the First Responders who serve our community. This is the most important work I have ever done in my life, and I am deeply thankful for you.

Jayme Johnston
Martha Buford
Erika Ramon
Joella Ballesteros
Priscilla Rodriguez
Mimo Alejandro
Melissa Petit
Jennifer Haby
Kathleen Maxwell-Rambie

Willie Balderas*
Veronica Gracia*
Stephen S.*
Adam-David Stephenson*
Paul Buford*
Samantha Diaz*
Juan Martinez*
Matt Caudillo*

*UFRST Peer Support *(you get a star)*

INTRODUCTION

So, we don't know each other. I only know that you have picked up this book and, for the moment, you're reading it. I appreciate that; talking about PTSD is my thing. This is the third book in our PTSD Recovery Series, and we've reached specialized communities around the world to talk about what PTSD is, what to do about it, and how to stay well.

Why a book for First Responders? Simply put, you need one. As a First Responder, you put your life on the line every day to help others in times of crisis. Whether you're a LEO, EMS, dispatcher, front-line medical, or military, you have the training and experience to be prepared for any emergency. Now, you have to focus on taking care of yourself *after the call.* Constant exposure to trauma and high-stress situations can have long-lasting effects on mental health.

I'm inviting you to take a knee and learn about PTSD for yourself and your team. I know PTSD is challenging, and I realize you may not be up to reading a book - but maybe you could try this one. I've worked in community mental health with First Responders for the last three years, and this is an important challenge to tackle.

I'm a mental health professional now, but a Soldier first. After my third deployment, I was definitely not okay and nobody knew how to help me – my Chain of Command, my doctors, my family, or me. I worked hard to get better, and I made lots of mistakes along the way. Eventually, I got my master's degree in mental health counseling, and I started teaching troops. I am convinced that when we know the facts about PTSD, we make more informed choices and get better faster. I am going to teach you everything I wish I knew when I started my own journey.

I am going to write this book directly to you, as if you were sitting in my class. My classes can feel uncomfortable; PTSD is an unpleasant topic and people don't like to talk about it. I get that, but that's not good for us. Your life is at stake, my friend, and I intend to be as straightforward as I know how.

There are a lot of great guides out there for civilians and clinicians, but this book is for First Responders. If someone had given me a book like this back in 2005 it would have saved me years of bull.

Very respectfully,

Virginia Cruse

TABLE OF CONTENTS

CHAPTER 1 PTSD RUMORS

First Responders put their lives on the line every day to help others in times of crisis. From law enforcement officers to paramedics, emergency dispatchers to military personnel, First Responders come from all walks of life and undergo extensive training to be prepared for any emergency. However, constant exposure to trauma and high-stress situations can have long-lasting effects on their mental health.

PTSD can develop in anyone after experiencing a trauma.
Trauma is defined as "actual or threatened exposure to death, serious injury, or sexual violence."

While these professionals are trained to maintain emotional control in order to effectively aid victims, the weight of each trauma they experience adds up over time.

Think of it like carrying a backpack filled with rocks, with each rock representing a traumatic event. As these brave men and women progress through their careers, their load becomes heavier and more difficult to bear.

How much can someone carry?

The weight will be different for each individual, as is how much each individual is capable of carrying.

No two people will experience the same stressful or traumatic situation in the same way.

Our experiences and ability to cope are as individual as we are, so trying to compare traumas is like comparing apples to sports cars.

That said, here are some facts:

- Over 80% of First Responders regularly experience traumatic events while working.
- 30% of First Responders develop behavioral health conditions including, but not limited to, depression and post-traumatic stress disorder (PTSD), compared with 20% in the general population.
- Emergency Medical Services (EMS) workers are 1.39 times more likely to commit suicide than the general population.
- In law enforcement, the estimates suggest between 125 and 300 police officers commit suicide every year.[1][2]

As First Responders, these traumas are a regular part of your job. And because that job title is "Hero," it's understandable that you might feel you can't show weakness, fear, or shame because that would be like admitting you don't have what it takes to do the job anymore.

Real Talk: That's a false narrative. One that needs to be obliterated.

And it's exactly why this book exists. It's time to dispel the rumors, remove the stigma, reveal the traumas and triggers, and point out the ways for you to access the help you need.

PTSD Rumors that are absolutely not true and mess with your head!

There's a lot of information about PTSD, but most of what's out there isn't user friendly. That's because most of what is written is by clinicians for clinicians using psychobabble that reads like IKEA furniture building instructions. It's meant to help those who help others, and while well-intentioned, it isn't easily digestible for the rest of us.

That's one of the biggest reasons the PTSD rumor mill is so powerful. If you aren't able to access the information you need, in a format that makes sense, the only thing you're left with is hearsay.

THE SKINNY

Post means "after"

Trauma is exposure to death, serious injury, or sexual violence.

Stress is your body's psychological and physical reaction to danger.

Disorder is a clinical word that means your symptoms are getting in the way of your walking, talking, everyday life.

Rumors will mess with your head and keep you from getting the treatment you deserve, so we're going to start off by dispelling a few of the big ones.

Why? Because, "Knowing is half the battle!"

We compiled this list of untruths from folks with PTSD, and from actual masters and doctoral level clinicians whose jobs are to treat PTSD. So, if you heard one of these and believed it was true, you're in good company.

RUMOR 1

"PTSD Has No Treatment."

Add to this, "I'll always have PTSD," "I'll never get better," and, "The symptoms may go away, but the PTSD will always be there."

These are powerful beliefs so widely held that many folks give up before getting started.

FACT: There are several Evidence-Based Treatments (EBTs) that have been shown to reduce PTSD symptoms, and the list of EBTs grows every year. In this book, we'll discuss some of the EBTs most widely available like:

- Prolonged Exposure Therapy
- Cognitive Processing Therapy
- Eye-Movement Desensitization and Reprocessing Therapy

All three of the above-mentioned EBTs have been proven to work for most people. (We will take a deep dive in Chapter 9.)

These treatment methods help with relaxation, reprocessing traumatic events, and reducing emotional distress.

When a therapy method is recognized as an EBT, it's a big deal.

Researchers conduct rigorous studies on these treatments using scientific methods, document their research in peer-reviewed scientific journals, and then other researchers conduct additional scientific studies to see if the treatment is, in fact, successful.

It's a lot like how drugs are tested by the FDA double-masked, randomized trials over a long period with lots of scrutiny.

STIGMA

We're going to go into more depth later (in Chapter 6), but since we're talking about rumors, we can't forget to mention one of the biggest things that contributes to PTSD or mental health rumors.

There is a fear among First Responders that being honest about their mental health struggles could harm their career prospects.[3]

On average, about one third of First Responders experience stigma regarding mental health issues, and First Responders across all professions under-report symptoms to avoid judgment, demotion, or a decrease in responsibilities at work. [4][5] More on this in Chapter 6.

For First Responders, trauma is part of the job. And seeking help is a necessary step to healing.

THE BOTTOM LINE

PTSD is treatable. EBTs work most of the time for most people. It doesn't matter how you feel. That's science. But hear this: Nothing and no one can convince you something is true if you strongly believe it is not. That's science, too.

RUMOR 2

PTSD is only for Military Service Members or "I don't deserve to have PTSD."

Let's start by making this crystal clear.

PTSD Can Develop In Anyone
Who Experiences Trauma.

It's not a merit badge. It's not a punch card. No one wants to develop PTSD. It is a serious condition brought about as the result of dealing with some pretty awful crap.

First Responders work in physically demanding settings characterized by traumatic events and personal danger, often coupled with environmental and occupational hazards. As a consequence of ongoing exposure to traumatic events, First Responders experience relatively high levels of depression and post-traumatic stress disorder (PTSD).[6]

TRAUMA COMPARISON

You can't talk about who deserves to have PTSD without bringing up trauma comparison.

Real talk: No one deserves to have the flu. But flu doesn't care about that. No one deserves to have malaria or HIV or schizophrenia, but we don't get a choice. PTSD is same-same.

Adding to that point, we need to understand that trauma comparison is not a valid gauge of individual experience.

TRUTH BOMB:

PTSD is something that happens to you, not something that is wrong with you.

No two people will experience the same stressful or traumatic situation in the same way.

What may traumatize one person may not feel that bad to another. Our experiences and our ability to cope are as individual as we are, so trying to compare traumas is like comparing apples to sports cars.

One of the EBTs for PTSD that focuses on "stuck points," or belief systems that keep us from getting better is **Cognitive Processing Therapy (CPT)**.

These may include:

- Intense guilt over all the victims they "should" have saved.
- Feeling like everyone close to them is going to get hurt.
- Not believing they make a difference.
- Losing faith in their career and becoming depressed as a result.

No one deserves to have PTSD, and we absolutely can come back from this.

RUMOR 3

*People who develop PTSD are "not resilient"
or "damaged goods."*

This is the idea that someone "gets" PTSD because they are not resilient enough, or because they already experienced trauma, addiction, etc. and are "damaged goods." This rumor equates PTSD to the flu and opines that PTSD attacks those with compromised mental immune systems.

> Trauma is an individual experience. What makes something traumatic for one person may not be traumatic for another, depending on their relative ability to deal with it.

It is fantasy to believe that a happy childhood will inoculate us from future trauma. It won't! There is no quick "bounce back" from exposure to serious trauma and pretending there is can have unintended consequences.

THE TRUTH ABOUT RESILIENCE

Resilience isn't something you're born with. It's the ability to persevere and overcome adversity.

That ability is built throughout a lifetime of experiences.

But being resilient does not mean that a person eliminates challenges or distress from their life. It means that they're able to adapt in the face of trauma, tragedy, and threats.

Remember that word, adapt. It's a verb, an action word. It means we have to *do* something.

To promote resilience within ourselves, we have to *develop* protective factors like exercise, a healthy diet, a healthy sleep schedule, good communication, and most important of them all, a healthy support network.

We may not always be able to sleep eight hours or eat healthy when on call. We may not be able to get in a good run or hit the gym. And for those reasons, those can't be the only strategies we turn to.

Resilience is active, right? So, what's the next item on our list?

When we're struggling and in need of help, we have to communicate our needs. And that's where having a healthy support network comes in.

As First Responders, you have to navigate and process some of the most difficult and traumatic situations imaginable…on a daily basis. There's not enough sleeping or eating right in the world that is going to fortify a person against the effects of trauma like that. To borrow a phrase, "It takes a village."

When there are people ready and willing to step in and help (peers, partners, friends, and/or family), you are better able to cope with difficult situations. Social support has been shown to reduce our level of stress during troubling situations. And knowing someone "has your back" creates the safe space you need to do the hardest thing possible. It allows you to reach out and ask for help when you need it.

Remember, resilience isn't just toughing it out through the worst situations. It's having a strategy and support system in place. And most importantly, using it when you need it.

It's important to know that those who have mental health conditions or experience symptoms can have positive outcomes with the right support.

But, if people in need of help feel they will be labeled as "weak" or "damaged," then they will be less likely to seek the help they need.

Not seeking help can have disastrous effects.

- Over 80% of First Responders report experiencing traumatic events on the job.
- 30% of First Responders develop behavioral health conditions including, but not limited to, depression and PTSD.
- It is estimated that 10–15% of First Responders have been diagnosed with PTSD.[7]
- First Responders made up 1% of all suicides from 2015 to 2017. When broken down by response discipline, these First Responder suicides occurred among law enforcement officers (58%), firefighters (21%), EMS providers (18%) and emergency medical dispatchers (2%).[8]

**Recognizing you need help
and reaching out for it is the bravest
thing you can do.**

Now that we know what PTSD is *not*, let's get down to brass tacks.

Read on.

CHAPTER 2 WHAT IS PTSD?

Post-Traumatic Stress Disorder is the result of exposure to trauma, where the symptoms of that trauma persist or get worse in the weeks and months after the traumatic event.

Not everyone who is exposed to trauma or traumatic events will develop symptoms of PTSD, but many will.

Common symptoms of PTSD include:

- Intrusive thoughts
- Avoiding reminders of the trauma
- Flashbacks
- Startling easily
- Hypervigilance
- Anxiety
- Irritability
- Self-destructive behavior
- Loss of interest in activities
- Emotional detachment
- An increased risk for suicide[9]

That is the simple explanation for a complicated disorder. We've got a lot to cover as we take a deep dive into PTSD. For now, you need to know that exposure to trauma is the root cause. Understanding is the first step in recovery.

FACT: There is only one way to get an official PTSD diagnosis, and that is with a licensed clinician who knows their DSM-5.

HOW IS TRAUMA DEFINED IN THE DSM-5?

The Diagnostic and Statistical Manual, Version Five (or Version Five Text Revision), should be on your therapist's bookshelf with the title *DSM-5* or *DSM-5-TR* on the spine.

The DSM-5 is the authoritative guide to the diagnosis of all mental disorders. It contains descriptions, symptoms, and criteria for diagnosis. Version five came out in 2013, and this is important for us to know in case we got a diagnosis before 2013.

> The clinical definition of PTSD changed significantly from version four to version five. If you see the gray DSM-IV or DSM-IV TR on your therapist's shelf: RUN.

The DSM is written by clinicians for clinicians. It has a lot of jargon and can be hard to understand.

To explain the facts of PTSD, we're going straight to the DSM-5 and providing a clinician-to-English translation.

When you discuss your PTSD with others, we want you to sound smart so that you can get the treatment you deserve and get your life back.

What Makes an Event Traumatic?

- It involves a threat—real or perceived—to one's physical or emotional well-being (Standard definition of trauma).
- It is overwhelming (Traumatic Stress).
- It results in intense feelings of fear and lack of control (Traumatic Stress).
- It leaves a feeling of helplessness (Traumatic Stress).
- It alters a person's perception of themselves, the world, and others (Moral Injury).

The current edition of the DSM-5 defines trauma as **actual or threatened exposure** to death, serious injury, or sexual violence.
This is important because human physiology does not differentiate between implied or physical harm.

Now that we know what exposure means, we need to understand how it applies, because that's where the expanded definition really helps us.

Traumatic Stress is the stress response to a traumatic event. Traumatic Stress falls into a few categories. First Responders deal with Traumatic Stress in more than one form. So, let's break this down.

Acute Stress Disorder (ASD) is a short-term mental health condition that can occur within the first month of experiencing a traumatic event. It involves stress responses, including anxiety, intense fear or helplessness, experiencing flashbacks or nightmares, feeling numb or detached from one's body, and avoiding situations, places or other reminders related to the traumatic event. ASD involves stress reactions that happen between three days and four weeks following a traumatic event.

Secondary Traumatic Stress (STS) was defined by Dr. Charles Figley.[10] It is the stress resulting from helping or wanting to help a traumatized or suffering person.

Vicarious Trauma is the negative effect of engaging empathetically with people who have directly experienced trauma, resulting in a state of tension and preoccupation arising from the trauma experiences described by clients.[11]

13

It is a theoretical term that focuses on the profound negative changes in a person's worldview due to the exposure to traumatic content of the people they help.[12]

Cumulative Trauma refers to the psychological, emotional, and physical distress associated with repeated exposure to traumatic events, either directly or indirectly. This cumulative exposure to traumatic stress throughout the First Responder's career causes ongoing distress, often referred to as sub-threshold post-traumatic stress disorder (S-PTSD).

You don't need physical scars to have trauma.

Understanding that simple statement leads to less stigma about trauma and better diagnosis and treatment options for those affected by it.

CHAPTER 3 TYPES OF TRAUMA

Before we dive into the technical parts of the DSM-5 and how it's used to diagnose and guide treatment for PTSD, we need to break down the various forms of trauma that affect First Responders.

COMPASSION FATIGUE

Compassion Fatigue was coined by Charles Figley in the 1980s and refers to a set of negative psychological symptoms that caregivers experience in the course of their work while being exposed to direct traumatic events or through Secondary Trauma.[13]

Within the context of First Responder's work, Compassion Fatigue is the stress resulting from exposure to traumatized individuals in the line of duty and the negative impact on your mental and physical health.

- Between 40% and 85% of helping professionals develop Vicarious Trauma, Compassion Fatigue and/or high rates of traumatic symptoms, according to Compassion Fatigue expert, Françoise Mathieu.[14]
- 86% of Nurses had moderate to high levels of Compassion Fatigue.[15]
- 15% of general practitioners turned to alcohol, prescription drugs or both to help them "deal with work pressures."[16]

- 33% of law enforcement showed high levels of emotional exhaustion and reduced personal accomplishment; 56.1 % scored high on the depersonalization scale.[17]
- Only 15% of law enforcement professionals were willing to seek personal counseling as a result of Vicarious Trauma versus 59% of mental health professionals.
- Estimated prevalence rates of 11% for PTSD, 15% for depression, 15% for anxiety, and 27% for general psychological distress amongst ambulance personnel.[18]

While not an exhaustive list, it definitely shows that those in the business of caring for others tend to be the most at risk.

Compassion Fatigue develops due to a combination of prolonged exposure to trauma or traumatized people and includes the inability to emotionally disengage from the suffering of others.

Personal Experience:

As EMS workers, we witness the pain and suffering that many people face every day, and not all of their stories have a happy ending. It's easy for everyday people to ignore or be unaware of the struggles that some individuals go through, but we are the ones who are called when things go wrong.

We come across cases of abuse, both physical and self-inflicted.

It's heart-wrenching to see individuals take advantage of the system for their own gain. And it's even more disheartening to visit the same residence multiple times in a short period for something as simple as helping someone stand up, knowing they are unable to live alone but have no other options.

There are also situations where individuals unknowingly destroy their own lives due to unhealthy habits and a refusal to make necessary changes. I've lost count of how many times I've responded to a call for difficulty breathing, only to find an elderly person relying on oxygen, surrounded by dingy walls and chain-smoking like it's their job.

After repeatedly experiencing these scenarios, it's natural to become jaded and disconnected from our emotions. To cope, I rely on my fellow paramedics. They're the only ones who I can unload on, because they understand the challenges we face on a daily basis.

Let's look at some of the risk factors which can be associated with Compassion Fatigue:

- A personal history of trauma.
- Being overworked, overwhelmed, and/or underpaid.
- Having limited professional experience and no training with Vicarious Trauma prevention.
- Working with a high percentage of traumatized children.
- Working under stressful conditions, with limited resources.

Compassion Fatigue is an erosive process. The negative effects of providing care are aggravated by the severity of the trauma which the First Responder is exposed to. The debilitating effects of Compassion Fatigue include exhaustion, anger and irritability, negative coping behaviors including alcohol and drug abuse, becoming emotionally detached or numb, and an impaired ability to make decisions and care for patients and/or clients. [19]

Dissociation, lack of concentration, as well as emotions like irritability and feelings of helplessness and hopelessness don't get left at work and also interfere with the individual's personal relationships.

Over time, Compassion Fatigue—often exacerbated by stress within the organization and a lack of recognition from the community—can make First Responders more susceptible to mental health issues, such as Depression, Burnout, and PTSD. The added pressure of public criticism and negative media coverage can further erode a First Responder's sense of support from the community and professional pride. This can further affect their overall ability to assist when encountering traumatic events in the line of duty.

Compassion Fatigue is more likely to occur if you're unaware of or ignore warning signs and do not seek help from resources like supervisors, peer-support groups, or clinical practitioners.

With that in mind, try to be aware of the following signs:

- Depression
- Frustration or Cynicism
- Feelings of uselessness
- Feeling disconnected from others
- Worries you're failing at your job
- Constantly feeling exhausted or tired
- Feeling the need to drink alcohol or do drugs

SECONDARY OR VICARIOUS TRAUMA

Secondary Trauma, also known as Vicarious Trauma, is a serious issue that can affect individuals who work in caregiving professions.

It is often used interchangeably with Compassion Fatigue, but there is a key difference between the two.

Compassion Fatigue is a gradual process of emotional and physical exhaustion caused by prolonged exposure to trauma while caring for others.

Secondary Trauma/Vicarious Trauma on the other hand, involves profound negative changes in an individual's worldview due to their exposure to traumatic content from those they are helping. [20] [21] They start to fear that the bad things they're exposed to will hurt them or their family if not constantly vigilant.

Personal Experience:

One of the hardest calls I had as a volunteer firefighter was at the beginning of my career. We were called to a heroin overdose, and when we arrived, the young man was completely unresponsive and blue. At the time, I was about the same age as him, and it felt surreal to be with his family in their lowest moment, knowing that this could happen to anyone at any time.

I tried to administer CPR, but his mouth was clenched shut and there was no way to get air into his lungs. His sister and brother were distraught and his mother was trying to convince us that if we could just get him to a doctor, he would be fine. But the reality was that he was gone.

It's easy for most of us to feel disconnected from situations like this until it becomes a possibility for us or someone we love. As a parent now, I am constantly scared by the thought that something like this could happen to my own child.

Compassion Fatigue and Vicarious Trauma may be a common occurrence in caregiving professions, but it doesn't have to take control of your life. By taking care of yourself and being aware of the warning signs, you can continue to provide excellent care without sacrificing your own well-being.

Be aware of the following problems:

- Fear in non-threatening situations.
- Physical symptoms including headaches, shortness of breath, and racing heart.
- Feeling others' trauma as if you experienced it yourself.
- Constantly feeling on guard or jumpy.
- Excessive fear that you, your colleagues, or loved ones may get hurt.
- Persistent intrusive thoughts involving the trauma of others.

During a TED Talk in 2017, Patricia Smith, the founder of the Compassion Fatigue Awareness Project, had this to say: [22]

"Caregivers are not good at asking for help. Asking for help is hard, no matter who you are. For nurses, doctors, teachers and more, the idea of leaving work can seem like an impossibility.

"You may feel guilty or that you are abandoning your patients or students. But if you are struggling with drug or alcohol use, you need help too. Your clients, patients and students will be happy for you."

CUMULATIVE TRAUMA

Caring for others is a noble calling, but it comes with its own set of challenges. Even with the necessary training and preparation, regularly facing traumatic situations can increase the risk for mental health issues.

> The toll of repeated exposure to traumatic events is referred to as Cumulative Trauma, and, if ignored, can have devastating effects on your well-being.

The psychological, emotional, and physical distress associated with repeated exposure to traumatic events, either directly or indirectly, can cause ongoing distress, often referred to as Sub-Threshold Post-traumatic Stress Disorder (S-PTSD).[23]

S-PTSD symptoms include irritability, sleep disruption, fatigue, anger, detachment, isolation, alcohol use increase, hypervigilance, startling, physical aches & pains, headaches, and anxiety. Diminished quality of life can be ongoing and can contribute to a higher incidence of PTSD.

Police Complex Spiral Trauma (PCST) is another term that addresses the cumulative impact of trauma experienced by LEOs over time due to the frequent exposure to traumatic events.[24]

As First Responders, you must maintain emotional control in order to effectively help those in need. However, this means you may not have the chance to fully process your own reactions and emotions while caring for others.

Personal Experience:

The majority of my job involves dealing with death and fatalities. Whether it's decapitation or severed limbs, I've grown accustomed to it. How you react to every call is different for every call. Adrenaline kicks in and I move into action without skipping a beat.

Older people affect you less than the younger ones. Fatalities are far worse than natural deaths. There could quite literally be body parts surrounding me and blood everywhere but no matter how gruesome the scene may be, seeing a child suffering, in pain, or deceased.... That stuff will stick with you.

After the call ends is when emotions and rethinking and replaying take over.

Reactions to situations, bad or good, are a natural part of being a human. However, constant exposure to traumatic or stressful situations, without acknowledging or working through the experiences, is where the signs of Cumulative Trauma begin showing up.

Indicators of Cumulative Trauma:

- Difficulty concentrating and frequent headaches
- Issues with sleep
- Becoming anxious or depressed
- Social withdrawal
- Relationship tension or problems
- Low motivation
- Alcohol or drug use problems
- Disciplinary problems at work
- Thoughts of self-harm

The list above is not an all-inclusive list, but if you are experiencing any of the symptoms, please seek help.

BURNOUT

The term Burnout was coined in the 1970s by the American psychologist Herbert Freudenberger.[25] He used it to describe the consequences of severe stress and high ideals in helping professions.

In 2019 the WHO International Classification of Diseases defined Burnout as:

> A syndrome conceptualized as resulting from chronic workplace stress that has not been successfully managed.

Burnout is much more complicated than ordinary fatigue. It is a state of emotional, physical, and mental exhaustion caused by excessive, prolonged stress.

A recent *What Firefighters Want* survey asked more than 2100 firefighters about their stress. On a scale of 1-10, approximately 76% of firefighters rated their stress level between 6 and 10, with 8 being the most common answer.

- 47% stated that stress from the job is negatively impacting relationships with family.
- 50% stated that stress is negatively impacting their ability to engage in hobbies, vacations, etc.
- 67% state that stress levels are negatively impacting their ability to sleep, time to exercise, etc.
- 42% of respondents stated that their stress level has caused them to consider leaving the fire service.[26]

Being burned out is characterized by three dimensions: 1) feelings of energy depletion or exhaustion; 2) increased mental distance from one's job, or feelings of cynicism related to one's job; and 3) reduced professional efficacy.[27]

Personal Experience:

In my previous line of work, I was called out to many disturbing events. However, one particular memory still haunts me to this day.

I was in an inner-city neighborhood with narrow streets and parked cars on both sides. A mother and her little boy had been sitting on their front stoop as the father pulled up and parked across the street. The boy saw his dad and excitedly ran towards him, between two parked cars.

Unfortunately, a woman was driving down the street at that moment, and didn't have enough time to see the child or react.

There was no chance for a miracle or for the child to be rushed to the ER. He was gone, just like that. And the fact that I knew both parents had witnessed the death along with the lady who accidentally killed that precious little boy. It's just haunting.

The image of that innocent little boy lying in the street has stayed with me ever since. I often dream about being back in that moment, trying to prevent the tragedy from happening. Sometimes I'm there before the accident and warn the mother to hold her son's hand. Other times, I'm the one sitting on the stoop with the boy instead of his mother.

That experience was what ultimately led me to quit my job. The pay wasn't enough to make up for the emotional toll.

Psychologists Herbert Freudenberger and Gail North have outlined the 12 phases of this stress syndrome:[28]

- **The Compulsion to Prove Oneself**
  Feeling like you constantly have to demonstrate your worth.

- **Excessive Drive/Ambition**
  Too much ambition can lead to Burnout. Ambition pushes a person to work harder.

- **Neglecting Needs**
  Begin to sacrifice self-care like sleep, exercise, and eating well.

- **Displacement of Conflict**
  Blaming the boss, the demands of the job, or colleagues for personal troubles.

- **No Time for Non-Work-Related Needs**
  Begin to withdraw from family and friends.

- **Denial**
  Impatience with others, seeing them as incompetent, lazy, or overbearing.

- **Withdrawal**
  Further pulling away from family and friends. Social invitations to parties, movies, and dinner feel burdensome.

- **Behavioral Changes**
  Those on the road to Burnout may become more aggressive and snap at loved ones for no reason.

- **Depersonalization**
  Feeling detached from life and the ability to enjoy it.

- **Inner Emptiness or Anxiety**
  Potential to turn to thrill-seeking behaviors, substance use, gambling, or overeating to cope with feelings.

- **Depression**
  Life loses its meaning. Extreme hopelessness.

- **Mental or Physical Collapse**
  Mental health care or medical attention may be necessary.

Burnout is not caused by stress alone. Here are some of the other factors that can lead to Burnout:

- Feeling like you have little or no control over your work.
- Lack of recognition or reward for good work.
- Unclear or overly demanding job expectations.
- Working too much, without enough time for socializing or relaxing.
- Lack of close, supportive relationships.
- Taking on too many responsibilities, without enough help from others.

As of the writing of this book, Burnout is not listed as a diagnosis in DSM-5.

People experiencing Burnout often can't see a way to change their situation. If not addressed and treated, Burnout can lead to a full-on mental health crisis.

Ask yourself these four questions to determine if you are suffering from Burnout:

1. How often are you tired and lacking energy to go to work in the morning?
2. How often do you feel physically drained, like your batteries are dead?
3. How often is your thinking process sluggish or your concentration impaired?
4. How often do you feel emotionally detached from co-workers (or customers) and unable to be sensitive to their needs?

MORAL DISTRESS

Moral Distress is a form of psychological pain that arises when an individual is expected to make the right decision, but is unable to do so due to an internal or external factor.

Moral Distress profoundly threatens a person's core values. This distress can accumulate over time and lead to feelings of helplessness, powerlessness, shame, compromised integrity and justice, reduced sense of dignity, and emotional suffering.[29]

It was defined by Andrew Jameton in the 1980s to describe the mental and moral stress experienced by nurses prevented from providing proper care due to institutional restrictions.[30] According to Jameton:

> "Moral Distress arises when one knows the right thing to do, but institutional constraints make it nearly impossible to pursue the right course of action."

It was first recognized among nurses, and the majority of studies have focused on this population.[31] [32] [33]

Moral Distress is particularly prevalent in disaster response situations. Here, responders are exposed to unsafe environments and overwhelming workloads.

In these situations, existing ethical guidelines might not be equipped to handle the complexity and pressure of the disasters or may not address the needs of First Responders on scene.[34]

Some Moral Distress examples for First Responders:

- A police officer, for reasons beyond their control, is not able to apprehend a dangerous criminal.[35]
- A fire crew on a hose line is instructed to evacuate before the primary search team has confirmed whether there are victims in the structure.
- A paramedic who is directed to provide treatment to a patient that goes against their belief on what's medically appropriate.[36]
- An EMS provider struggling with their moral responsibility to provide care when a patient denies treatment or transport regardless of medical advice.[37]

The key element in Moral Distress is the individual's feeling of powerlessness and their inability to carry out what they believe is ethically right.

Personal Experience

As a former 911 dispatcher, I often felt helpless while listening to distressing calls. My main responsibility was to get the right resources to the scene with accurate information, but it took a toll on me emotionally.

The most difficult calls were the ones where I couldn't get a good location. One of my first calls, during my training, was from a father who had been four-wheeling with his son and some friends.

Unfortunately, his son crashed into a tree and was not breathing. The father knew where they had entered the woods, but they had driven too far for him to know their current location.

While sending help to the last known area, I tried to obtain a better location cell tower ping, and walked him through performing CPR on his child.

My instructor said I handled it well, but personally, I was in a dark place afterward. I had just become a parent myself, so it hit close to home. Sadly, the child didn't make it.

There is no way of knowing if a quicker response could have saved him or not... and that's something you never fully come to terms with.

Moral Distress is a significant threat to an individual's core values, leading to a sense of inner turmoil and damaging their moral integrity.

Over time, this distress can accumulate and result in feelings of helplessness, shame, compromised ethical standards, and emotional pain.[38]

External constraints that contribute to Moral Distress include:

- Power imbalances (between members of the healthcare or responder team)
- Poor communication (between team members)
- Pressure to reduce costs
- Fear of legal action
- Lack of administrative support
- Policies that conflict with patient care needs

Moral Distress can occur in two stages: "initial distress" at the time of the issue and "reactive distress" later on. Even after the reactive stress subsides, it may leave behind a lasting impact known as "moral residue," which can have a cumulative negative effect on mental well-being.

One of the main challenges in addressing Moral Distress is identifying it in the first place.

This psychological suffering can also manifest into physical symptoms and contribute to chronic illnesses:

- New or worsening headaches, heart palpitations, & gastric upset
- Lingering anger
- Feelings of guilt or shame
- Withdrawal and depression

If you suspect you may be experiencing Moral Distress, it is important to identify, assess, and address it.

The presence of Moral Distress is a sign that ethical challenges are not being addressed adequately.

MORAL INJURY

In the 1990s, the term "Moral Injury" was coined by psychiatrist Jonathan Shay and colleagues and defined it as,[39]

"A betrayal of what is right by someone who holds legitimate authority in a high stakes situation."

In 2009, the term "Moral Injury" was modified by Brett Litz and colleagues, adding:[40]

"Perpetrating, failing to prevent, or bearing witness to acts that transgress deeply held moral beliefs and expectations."

In simple terms, Moral Injury means acting in a way (witnessing, participating, or failing to prevent something) that goes against a person's moral beliefs. These "transgressive acts" violate an individual's acceptable boundaries of behavior.

While Moral Injury research has mainly focused on military Service Members and Veterans, it is gradually gaining recognition as a significant and widespread issue among First Responders.[41]

This is not surprising considering the constant exposure to traumatic events that comes with their job.[42]

As professionals in bureaucratic systems, First Responders must follow strict codes of conduct, adhere to standards of practice, and follow the law when making decisions. The unpredictable and potentially traumatic nature of First Responders' work often requires them to make split-second decisions in high-stress situations where their safety and that of others are on the line. And those decisions may go against their personal morals.

Scenarios that could lead to Moral Injury:[43] [44]

- A firefighter being unable to save a victim or having to choose between victims to save.
- A law enforcement officer having to use physical or lethal force to resolve a criminal incident.
- A paramedic having a patient die en route to the hospital, or finding out that their patient died after arriving at the hospital.
- Being forced to make difficult decisions about how to allocate resources during a crisis.
- Making a mistake that led to the death of a colleague.
- A fellow First Responder dying by suicide.

Moral Injury is not classified as a mental illness by the DSM-5, but a 2018 meta-analysis found that exposure to potentially morally injurious events were significantly associated with Post-Traumatic Stress Disorder, depression, and suicidality.[45]

Moral Distress and Moral Injury may appear to be very similar since both are related to moral suffering. However, what appears to mainly distinguish Moral Injury from Moral Distress is that Moral Injury refers to the moral dilemmas where violence and death occur.

Moral Injury is a deep suffering because, in a high-stakes situation, something went wrong and either the First Responder couldn't prevent it or was forced to cause harm to another human being. The pain itself is a sign of a working conscience responding to devastating conditions.

First Responders who are more spiritual are also more likely to experience distress, possibly due to the clash between their religious beliefs (e.g., "Thou shall not kill") and their actions in the line of duty. For law enforcement officers who have killed or severely injured a perpetrator in the line of duty, they are at higher risk of developing PTSD if they do not address their Moral Injury.[46]

Moral Injury challenges our fundamental core values, it eats away at us, and undermines the trust we have in ourself, in others, and in the world we live in.

3 CATEGORIES OF MORAL INJURY

Loss in the line of duty.

We make unique bonds when save lives together, and we can feel personally responsible for the safety of everyone in the unit. When someone dies in the line of duty, it feels like a failure. There is seldom a chance to mourn because the mission must go on, and we have to swallow our feelings of failure (no matter how the death occurred).

It's hard to square conflicting feelings. We use words like "hero" and "sacrifice," but what does that mean when our colleague is dead and not coming back?

We could question the value of the mission, the corruption of our leadership, or whether it really had to go down that way. Even thinking this way can make us feel as if we are dishonoring our buddy, so we swallow it instead.

Perpetration.

Perpetration is a big umbrella, and it's hardly simple. It includes what we believe we did, what we believe we didn't do, or what we believe we "should have known" would happen. Notice that word, "believe." Moral Injury messes with our fundamental belief systems, and perpetration includes, but is not limited to, accidental or intentional killing and/or failure (either real or perceived) to prevent the death of someone.

Leadership Betrayal.

Everyone makes mistakes. That's a given. Acts that fall into this category of "Leadership Betrayal" are behaviors that are especially capricious, risky, and entail wholly unfair treatment. The consequences can be horrific because toxic leaders thrive in chaotic situations with little oversight. In situations of Leadership Betrayal, "leaders" violate all reasonable expectations of moral and ethical conduct, and it is highly unlikely there will be justice because that is not how life works.

First Responders have a multitude of responsibilities, including advocating for patients, providing social services, enforcing laws, and protecting the community. As professionals in bureaucratic systems, First Responders must follow strict codes of conduct, uphold implicit duties, and adhere to standards of practice and the law when making decisions.

The unpredictable and potentially traumatic nature of their work often requires First Responders to make split-second decisions.

These decisions are often made in high-stress situations where their own safety and that of others is on the line and may go against their personal morals.

Even if a First Responder's actions don't violate their morals at the time, an unfavorable outcome such as the death of a victim or serious injury to a team member can lead to feelings of remorse and Moral Injury.[47] [48]

Journalist Diane Silver describes Moral Injury as, "*A deep soul wound that pierces a person's identity, sense of morality, and relationship to society.*"[49]

Litz et al.'s research found that we punish ourselves by sabotaging or "self-handicapping."[50]

We can't talk about it, so we isolate. We stuff our feelings down, jump into a bottle, and become our own most vicious critic.

The self-talk is debilitating.
"*Only a monster would ____*"
"*Only an animal would ____*"
"*It should have been me.*"

We fill in that blank and play it over and over in our minds.

With Moral Injury, the trauma
and its meaning need to be processed.

We need to stare into the belly of the beast and process betrayal, anger, self-loathing, and the desire to self-harm.

Signs of Moral Injury:

- Feeling demoralized
- Feeling guilt/shame
- Feeling "haunted" by decisions, actions or inactions that have been made
- Anger in particular following betrayal
- Feelings of worthlessness, helplessness, and powerlessness
- Questioning our sense of self and a loss of trust in oneself and in others
  Persistent self-blame, negative beliefs, and self-condemnation
- Self-isolation, avoidance, and withdrawal from others
- Reduced empathy or wanting to interact with others
- Increase in substance use
- Loss of spirituality or religious beliefs (if previously held)
- Suicidal ideation

If you feel you are suffering from Moral Injury, please seek support and professional help.

INSTITUTIONAL BETRAYAL

Institutional Betrayal is a serious issue that occurs when an institution or organization violates the trust and loyalty of those who rely on it.

Jennifer J. Freyd, PhD is the Professor Emerit of Psychology at the University of Oregon who coined the term in 2008 and has conducted extensive research on it.[51]

This includes any failure to prevent or appropriately respond to wrongdoings perpetrated by members of, or within, the institution.

Institutional Betrayal is a systemic issue that runs rampant in our modern society and comes in many nuanced flavors that can contribute to or exacerbate trauma.

It may be systemic, such as an institution lacking protective work policies, or isolated, such as a colleague taking credit for another's work. It can happen through actions (like retaliating against an employee who speaks out about bullying) or lack of action (like not telling an employee about their rights under FMLA when their child is seriously ill).[52]

Institutional Betrayal is more likely to occur within organizational structures with embedded prestige that resist change. People who are attached and dependent on the organization may not want to quit their job, leave school, or remove themselves from the church or their community.

This is especially true when the affiliation is an essential element of the individual's identity. If you leave, you are no longer a firefighter, police officer, or healthcare provider.

In cases of workplace abuse, betrayal becomes part of how the institution operates.

This may look like a rookie firefighter who repeatedly reports the bullying behavior of several colleagues to their chief. But instead of addressing the concern, the reports are dismissed without investigation. Desperate for help, the rookie firefighter reaches out again and, in this case, when they attempt to accuse their aggressor, the result is humiliation or ostracization, rather than punishment for the aggressor.

This flipping of scripts is a common tactic in workplace abuse and is an example of DARVO "Deny, Attack, Reverse Victim & Offender, "an aggressive form of Institutional Betrayal. [53]

The effects of Institutional Betrayal can be likened to emotional abuse in close relationships—often more damaging than abuse from a stranger. The breach of trust, lack of loyalty, and potential for retaliation are like a knife in the back. And because they are bound to the system in which the betrayal occurred, there is often an internalization of this pain.

As a coping mechanism, individuals may repress and deny their trauma, leading to anxiety and disruptions in memory and awareness. According to Smith and Freyd, these adaptive strategies, "allow for the maintenance of necessary relationships (even abusive ones) in a way that supports attachment behaviors."

On the outside, this looks like acceptance, leaving the betraying behavior to continue.

A study in the United States, *Reflections on the lived experience of working with limited personal protective equipment during the COVID-19 crisis,* reported that many nurses lacked paid leave during their mandatory 2- to 3-week quarantines, which fostered a sense of betrayal toward their organization.[54]

Organizational cultures that normalize abusive behavior, ignore reports of problems, and retaliate against whistleblowers tend to exhibit high instances of Bureaucratic Cruelty/Administrative Betrayal.

BUREAUCRATIC CRUELTY

Bureaucratic Cruelty, sometimes called Administrative Betrayal can involve acting badly or not acting at all, and it can also vary in terms of whether it is "apparently isolated" or "apparently systemic." This includes institutional tolerance for bad acts, investigations lacking transparency, untimely complaint resolution, inadequate or inconsistent sanctions, and other forms of effective indifference. This is especially damaging to personal and professional well-being.

Some examples of Bureaucratic Cruelty/Administrative Betrayal:[55]

- When the issues of Moral Distress and Compassion Fatigue are not addressed within organizations that routinely deal with trauma.
- An officer shot and killed a suspect who was randomly shooting at people, including himself, was asked to write a letter of apology to the dead suspect's family in hopes the letter would avoid a lawsuit.
- After being injured on the job, an officer's workers compensation claim was rejected. He turned to his employer for help and was told there was nothing anyone could do.
- Failing to protect a First Responder from the press and allowing private observations to be publicly recorded.
- Witnessing unethical behavior or actions by fellow First Responders or superiors.
- Mandatory overtime due to staff shortages.
  Vacation time is no longer protected due to staff shortages.
- Witness discrimination or harassment within the organization or towards members of the public.

- Witnessing or participating in behavior that violates a sense of ethics or morality, such as hazing or harassment.
- Stigma of the "culture" of First Responders. For example, firefighters are often expected to be stoic and unemotional in the face of danger, leading to reluctance to seek help when experiencing psychological distress.
- Feeling pressure to conform to a certain image of being a "good" First Responder, which can lead to feelings of inadequacy or shame if they do not live up to these expectations.

Talking about shifting the culture to one of mental wellness but not acting on it is another form of Administrative Betrayal that is coming under scrutiny recently.

Personal Experience:

Got into therapy after a horrific incident at work that I couldn't shake and I ended up going for a year of weekly sessions. It was crucial to find an outlet to release the weight of my experiences, because 15 years of keeping it bottled in almost led me to retire early. Even finding a therapist familiar and comfortable with our field proved difficult.

I ended up asking a close friend that does our debriefings and they provided some names but none were seeing new patients.

I eventually resorted to seeking out a specialist online, paying out of pocket until it became unsustainable. It shouldn't be this challenging to find support in our field.

Feelings of being unappreciated, frustration, anger, and disappointment lead to distrust and a perception that their organization does not support them. In turn, the changes in attitude had negative effects on the First Responders' willingness to put effort into the organization and their work. Invalidation and lack of support from the organization leads to feelings of shame, failure, and an eroded self-worth.

"The message of health and wellness that is presented to the organization is in direct conflict with the actions of the organization. While there are individuals who are working hard and advocating for total wellness and moral/ethical support, the organization seems to only support the members if there is no real financial investment required or particular effort on behalf of the organization." *Wounds of the Spirit: Moral Injury in Firefighters.*[56]

MASS CASUALTY INCIDENTS (MCIS)

DISASTERS

Disasters, either man-made or natural, are Mass Casualty Incidents (MCIs) that have a significant detrimental effect on the physical and mental well-being of the exposed population. First Responders have a duty to act on such occasions and are likely to experience at least one, if not multiple events, in their career.

Moral Distress is particularly prevalent in disaster response situations. Here, responders are exposed to unsafe environments and overwhelming workloads. In these situations, existing ethical guidelines might not be equipped to handle the complexity and pressure of the disasters, or may not address the needs of First Responders on scene.[57]

First Responders who already work under dangerous conditions are at an increased risk of developing symptoms of PTSD in these high-stress environments.[58]

Incidents involving children, suicides, and grotesque mutilation are the most distressing.[59] A study on Emergency Medical Responders (EMRs) found that serious operational and physical demands were the most common severe stressors. Additionally, they had higher levels of emotional exhaustion and depersonalization. Over 13% of the EMRs in this study had PTSD. Emotional levels among EMRs with PTSD were significantly higher (42%) than those without PTSD (17%).[60]

Traumatic events, such as severe burns/injuries, suicide victims, or a child with unintentional injuries correlate with traumatic distress and PTSD symptoms of nurses who work in Emergency Departments (EDs).[61] Similarly, a study in the Netherlands showed that nearly one out of three nurses in EDs reported subclinical levels of depression, anxiety and somatic symptoms, with more than 8% meeting a clinical level of PTSD.[62]

Another study on German physicians in EDs reported that almost 8% of doctors had depressive symptoms, about 17% had probable PTSD, and more than 3% had clinical depressive symptoms.[63] Among Belgian emergency doctors, almost 15% had a clinical level of PTSD, about 11% had anxiety and almost 8% had depression after traumatic incidents.[64]

ACTIVE SHOOTER SITUATION

First Responders see and deal with many things that the average civilian could not handle. One crucial thing they do is to respond to the increasing number of active shooter tragedies.

These violent attacks and chaotic scenes often result in multiple critically injured persons and mass casualties.

In an active shooter situation, law enforcement officers (LEOs) are the first to enter the scene. Fire or emergency medical service (EMS) personnel cannot enter the incident scene until the situation is deemed safe, which means LEOs often encounter victims first but cannot stop to perform emergency medical lifesaving procedures while an active shooter is present.[65] [66]

Remember when we mentioned Moral Injury?

This is one of those cases.

It is the right course of action to secure the scene, find the shooter, and prevent more injuries. However, for that LEO facing a potentially dying person, the inability to help them in that moment can have lasting effects on their psyche.

Only when a shooter has been apprehended or the scene is deemed safe can EMS, fire, and search and rescue teams begin to assess, triage, and provide care to the injured.

GROUND ZERO

Whether a disaster or active shooter situation, ground zero—the central point of destruction or impact in a disaster—is a chaotic and overwhelming place to be, filled with potentially wounded, disoriented, confused, in shock, and scared people.

By this point, the immediate danger may have passed, but this is where the toll on mental health is intensified. Due to the nature of their work, First Responders must maintain emotional control in order to effectively help victims.

There is no time for First Responders to process their reactions or the emotions they're experiencing as they treat severely injured individuals, handle deceased bodies or body parts, comfort those who have lost loved ones, and cope with unsuccessful attempts to save victims.

Disaster–related factors that contribute to First Responder distress:

- Responding to a human–caused disaster, rather than a naturally occurring event.
- Feeling unsafe in the disaster zone.
- The development of an empathic attitude toward survivors.
- Experiencing helplessness in the disaster zone.
- The intensity of exposure to traumatic scenes.[67]

First Responder reports indicate that lack of control for the suffering of others is a critical factor in the amount and degree of distress they experience.[68]

> Handling the bodies of children has a universally disturbing effect on First Responders.

Responders tasked with clearing the site after the 2012 Century 16 movie theatre shooting in Aurora, Colorado reported that hearing the ringing of cellphones lying next to the deceased was very upsetting. Teams entering Columbine High School had to contend with the sight of dead and wounded children. LEOs who entered the Sandy Hook Elementary school not only had to contend with the horrific sights, they were also overwhelmed by the smell of gunpowder.[69]

Providing emergency psychological care has consistently been shown to reduce chronic mental illness in trauma survivors, and it is widely accepted that First Responders involved in MCIs require immediate support.

In these situations, First Responders should be provided with Psychological First Aid (PFA) as they process through the command center. PFA is a widely endorsed and promising evidence-informed early intervention model grounded in research on trauma recovery and resilience.

Findings from studies on PFA suggest it has a positive impact on survivors of MCIs and First Responders, with most reporting reduced symptoms of anxiety, depression, post-traumatic stress, as well as improved ratings of mood, the experience of safety, connectedness, and a sense of control.

The use of PFA was demonstrated at the Pentagon following the 9/11 attacks. There, multi-disciplinary teams provided initial triage, psychosocial support, and referral for further assessment and treatment, as well as leadership consultation to public health workers. This technique was also utilized at Columbine High School in Colorado.[70]

On a global scale, there has been a 10x increase in disasters since 1990 and disasters are predicted to continue increasing in frequency along with the demand for First Responders.

The incidence of psychological issues such as PTSD is also predicted to continue to rise as First Responders are exposed to more of these highly traumatic incidents.

It is vital that First Responders have the necessary mental health services to help them cope.

SHAME, TOXIC POSITIVITY, AND GUILT: THE TRAUMATIC TRIFECTA

SHAME

The culture of First Responder work emphasizes strength, self-reliance, and saving others above all else. This can create a stigma around seeking help for mental health issues, as many feel pressure to present themselves as unbreakable heroes. So even when they are struggling, many First Responders suffer in silence, afraid to be seen as weak or unfit for their job.[71]

But pushing aside emotions and burying pain can only exacerbate the emotional weight of the job. It leads to Burnout, isolation, and a sense of hopelessness.

Many First Responders are afraid to share their true experiences because they feel it is "too trivial," or they feel their pain is "unworthy" of burdening others. Some simply hide their pain for fear of the stigma associated with mental health issues in a culture where they are expected to "suck it up" because "this is what they signed up for."

They shut their feelings down and try to bury them. Isolation begins as they hide their shame.

> Burying feelings of trauma and shame only
> further entrenches them.

A personal favorite of mine, Dr. Brené Brown, who has spent decades studying courage, vulnerability, shame, and empathy, describes shame as:

"The intensely painful feeling or experience of believing that we are flawed and therefore unworthy of love and belonging — something we've experienced, done, or failed to do makes us unworthy of connection." [72]

In describing the difference between guilt and shame, Brown notes that guilt is, "I did something wrong." And shame is, "I am something wrong."[73]

She goes on to explain that all shame needs to grow is the destructive trio of silence, secrecy, and judgement.

Unfortunately, when many of us experience pain or suffering, we allow shame to force us into the silence.

> The more we try to avoid speaking about our
> problems, the more they negatively impact our lives.

This only leads to a deeper sense of loneliness and isolation.

Burnout, hopelessness, and mental health issues like anxiety, depression, and PTSD are just some of the consequences of neglecting mental health in this profession.

Yes, trauma is part of the job, but when it begins to take a toll, it has to be addressed.

The problem with failing to express and address pain, no matter how seemingly insignificant: it will find a way to seep into and negatively impact other areas of life. In effect, shame becomes a catalyst for more damage and destruction.

TOXIC POSITIVITY

We've mentioned that shame is the internal voice that tells us we are horrible, and a burden, and should keep our problems to ourselves. Well, there is an equally insidious "outside voice" version of this, too.

We call this Toxic Positivity. Rather than coming from within, this is the feedback we get from others, or what we tell ourselves, that reinforces our shame and prevents us from seeking help.

Toxic Positivity is a form of invalidation and falls into the category of gaslighting and emotional abuse.

Yeah, it can be that serious.

Instead of facing difficult emotions, Toxic Positivity rejects or ignores the negative, glossing over emotional pain with a cheerful, often falsely positive, facade.

This can come in the form of burying one's own feelings and avoiding anything negative, or it can come as a response to expressing those negative feelings with another person.

Common examples:

Feigning Gratitude or Praise.

Focusing on gratitude to bypass emotions. Gratitude is not a bad thing. Neither is praise. But they can be when used to invalidate or ignore your pain.

"Look on the bright side."

"Count your blessings."

"I just can't believe how strong you are. I'd never survive what you're going through. Keep up the good work."

Comparing.

Just because someone else is seemingly handling a tough time "better" than you, that's no reason to start comparing. Everyone handles things in their own way.

"You think you have it rough?"

"It could be worse."

"If I can do it, so can you."

Dismissing Difficult Emotions.

When difficult emotions arise, you completely push them down, insisting you must stay positive. It's a form of gaslighting.

"Everything happens for a reason."

"You signed up for this. Now suck it up and do your job."

"Failure is not an option."

A Toxic Positivity response creates a disconnect in a person's ability to rely on their social support structure. And the worst part is these responses can come from others, or they can come from your own mind.

First Responders, you are heroes, bravely risking your lives to save others. No doubt about that. You deal with trauma on a daily basis. And when on the job, you must maintain emotional control in order to effectively help those in need. Compartmentalizing emotions is a big part of that. And that's a mentally and physically demanding thing to do. But your dedication to prioritizing the safety and well-being of your community often means putting your own needs second.

Toxic Positivity is the bandage you put over feelings. You "suck it up," (or are told to) because that's what it takes to be a life saver.

You see peers doing just fine and berate yourself for feeling so bad. Or maybe you do mention you're feeling a bit out of sorts and the feedback is one of those phrases listed above. Pick your poison.

Any invalidating response, when someone reaches out for help, is going to shut that person down.

And that's what makes this so toxic.

Now, I'm not saying everything has to be heavy or serious all the time. Having a positive outlook on life is good for your mental well-being.

Trying to remain optimistic when times get tough can be good... up to a point. Practicing false cheerfulness, to avoid addressing feelings that are weighing us down, however, leaves negativity to fester and erode our mental health.

Toxic Positivity can cause serious harm to people who are

going through difficult times. Rather than being able to share their troubles and gain much-needed support, the invalidation of Toxic Positivity leaves people feeling dismissed and shamed, compounding the problems they're already dealing with.

Among the worst offenders of toxic positive responses, in my opinion, is false praise. Now, I might not be a First Responder, but I've endured my fair share of trauma. And like you, I avoid having to ask for help. But, when I've broken down and finally do reach out for help, I'm hoping the person I'm opening up to will be there for me. To have someone reply with something like, "I just admire how strong you are. I could never endure all you have. Keep up the good work, you'll get through it."

Hearing that is possibly worse than being told to shut up or suck it up. Not only is it a "no" on the help I've asked for, but it's also a special kind of knife twist because they're reminding me of how hard I have struggled while humble bragging about how easy their life is in comparison. It's not a true validation of the pain, nor an offer for help.

What do you say after that? Well, just like being told to "suck it up," when false praise comes back as your answer, there is only one thing to do:

You shut those feelings down and try to bury them. You push aside any of the bad feelings, the Compassion Fatigue, and the lingering sense of Burnout. You know you have only yourself, so you go within. Isolation begins. But feelings don't like to stay down. They will come up again.

You blame the bad mood that has become a permanent undercurrent of your personality on a bad call or a poor night of sleep. You look to your peers to see just how weak you are in comparison. Shame sets in.

This is where the stigma reinforces the idea that if someone is struggling, they might not have what it takes to do the job. You start gaslighting yourself.

"None of the others on the team seem to have problems. I just have to try harder. Suck it up. Don't be such a whiner. Things could be worse."

Talking about problems is taboo, so you don't want to burden anyone, including your loved ones, with your trivial feelings. You become avoidant of social situations because what's the point? Isolation becomes an additional part of your personality. You say it's because you don't want to drag everyone down with your mood, or you're just too tired after a long day.

Maybe you start self-medicating at the end of the shift to help raise your spirits. And for a while, maybe you think that's all you need. Alcohol numbs the pain a bit. Sleeping pills help you get more rest.

But the truth is, if you're self-medicating to help keep those buried feelings numb and isolating from your support network, you're already half-way down the slippery slope.

You can't ignore trauma, and there is no way to think it away with happy thoughts.

You have to address it, or the problem will get worse. It's not a weakness to ask for help. And if you have asked and been treated to some Toxic Positivity for your trouble, I'm sorry. But you have to try again.

Reach out to your support network, close friends, family,

and your partner. The people who love you will not see your problems as a burden. They want to see you healthy.

People going through trauma don't need to be told to stay positive, they need empathy.

When someone is suffering, they need to know that their emotions are valid, and they can find relief and love in their friends and family.

GUILT

Survivor's Guilt is the shame of being the one who lived.

One of the most significant causes of First Responder trauma is guilt.

This is often linked to Compassion Fatigue or high levels of empathizing with victims, but the guilt often comes from feeling helpless or even shame over surviving.

The simple fact is that First Responders encounter death in the course of their work.

Personal Experience:

Early in my career, I took a call for a child who had fallen into a pool. There were actually two kids who had wandered out of their home. The little girl was found floating in the shallow end of the neighbor's pool. No sight of the little boy.

The dad had gotten the little girl out of the pool and was desperately trying CPR when we arrived. Still hadn't found the little boy. I took over CPR. The father disappeared. Suddenly I heard him wailing. He'd found the little boy in the deep end of the neighbor's pool. Guess the little boy had been there that whole time the father was trying to save his little girl. Both of the kids died that day.

Unfortunately, this wasn't the first or last time I would respond to a drowning call involving children.

Now that I have kids of my own, anytime they are around a pool, I'm always on high alert. I just can't relax.

My family even sometimes avoids inviting me to events with pools, which is probably for the best. Even though I don't experience flashbacks, it's impossible not to be reminded of all the drowning calls I've been on. As a father, I constantly worry about the safety of my own children near water because I have seen how quickly it can take life away.

When there's an emergency, First Responders are the ones heading to the action, actively trying to prevent the loss of life or a traumatic outcome. They're faced with harrowing scenarios such as car accidents, mass casualties, and building fires where they cannot save everyone.

Survivor's Guilt is a difficult emotion to navigate through, especially for First Responders, because they're more inclined to experience a heightened amount of traumatic events compared to the general population.

Be aware of the signs.

If someone is expressing any of the following thoughts or

making these comments after a traumatic event, that person may be struggling with Survivor's Guilt:

"I don't deserve help when someone else needs it more than me."

"I keep thinking if only I had…"

"I feel like there was more I could have done."

"I should have…"

"Why was I the one that survived?"

"I'm so angry at myself for not trying harder."

"How can I be happy when all those others who died cannot?"

"Why should I enjoy life experiences when they can't?"

Survivor's Guilt can take the form of a firefighter feeling guilty about not being able to save a life while risking their own in the blaze of fire, an EMT whose patient dies on route to hospital, or a police officer whose partner, standing inches away, took a bullet that was meant for them.

Feeling lucky to be alive is an emotion many of us might not associate with guilt. Some may not even realize they are experiencing it, or they struggle to recognize that the weight they are carrying alongside their grief is actually a sense of guilt.

When faced with loss or trauma, this guilt can consume us, leading to self-destructive coping mechanisms such as substance abuse.

We may also feel unworthy of receiving help and finding happiness after experiencing such pain when others could not. It's almost as if we feel we owe the world something for being alive.

But what many don't realize is that holding onto this guilt

can be harmful to our well-being.

We all deserve the chance to live a fulfilling life, regardless of what happened in the past.

As with Shame and Toxic Positivity, you can't ignore the feelings. You have to address them or the problem will get worse.

When someone is suffering, they need to know that their emotions are valid, and they can find relief and love in their friends and family.

ISOLATION AND LOSS OF SOCIAL SUPPORT

In today's world, we often overlook loneliness and isolation as trivial concerns. But the truth is, these are critical symptoms of an eroded social support network that can have serious impacts on our physical and mental health.

For First Responders, this issue hits even closer to home. The nature of their work—constantly facing life-threatening situations, dealing with trauma, and maintaining unpredictable schedules—can take a toll on their personal lives. It becomes challenging to nurture and sustain meaningful relationships when their duties consume so much of their time and energy.

But why is this worth listing in the trauma section?

Research has shown that social support not only helps us cope with tough times but also plays a vital role in promoting mental wellness.[74]

Lack of social support, however, is a major factor contributing to feelings of hopelessness and suicide among First Responders.[75]

> When we lack social support, we become more vulnerable to experiencing symptoms of depression, PTSD, anxiety, and other psychiatric disorders.

All of which are already prevalent among First Responders.

So, what exactly causes this sense of loneliness and isolation among First Responders? One major factor is the breakdown of close relationships or losing people from one's support network. Additionally, stigma surrounding mental health issues often discourages First Responders from seeking help.

Let's look at some of these items a little closer.

BREAKDOWN OR LOSS OF FRIENDSHIPS

As First Responders enter their career, they often have a close-knit group of friends that is separate from their work peers.

But as they become more immersed in the demands of their job, they may find themselves sacrificing personal time and hobbies in order to fulfill their duty. This can lead to a natural distance between friends, making it difficult to maintain a strong social life.

However, studies have shown the importance of maintaining a social network for First Responders.

Those with larger networks and strong social support tend to experience less stress and better mental health overall. This concept, known as the "stress-buffering hypothesis," suggests that having a strong support system can help reduce negative thoughts and beliefs following a traumatic experience. [76]

But for many First Responders, maintaining these friendships can be challenging. Their demanding schedules and confidentiality obligations make it hard to connect with friends who haven't experienced similar situations. There is also a sense that others may not fully understand what they've been through, leading to a feeling of disconnection.

Despite these challenges, these friendships are crucial for First Responders because they offer an outlet outside of work.

These friendships, though somewhat disconnected, are vital because they provide camaraderie that allows the First Responder to fully disengage from the stress and trauma experienced on the job.

Schedule difficulties aside, time and effort to maintain these friendships are essential or they will dwindle. And that means losing important social support outside of the workplace.

A healthy social network includes variety, so while our first set of friends is crucial, we can't discount the importance of peers and work friends—brothers and sisters on your team.

The bond First Responders share is like no other. The things they go through and see together help them feel understood and often distant from others.

It's common for First Responders to slowly see their original friend group narrow as their work friends increase, but both are equally vital.

These friendships provide camaraderie that allows the First Responder to feel understood through the stress and trauma experienced on the job.

But though the bond between peers is unique in its forged-through-fire strength, it can quickly disappear when the individual is no longer a part of the day-to-day of the department due to leave, transfers, injuries, early retirements, etc.

The circle a First Responder surrounds themselves with at work can sometimes be a false sense of security. This is because dealing with trauma means one can never know what the next shift might bring, and losses on the job are not uncommon.

This is why it's essential for First Responders to intentionally build a large social network both inside and outside of their workplace.

First Responders have to navigate and process some of the most difficult and traumatic situations imaginable... on a daily basis. There's not enough sleeping or eating right in the world that is going to fortify a person against the effects of trauma like that. To borrow a phrase, "It takes a village."

When relationships break down or dwindle, so too does the protection that the social network provides.

Poor social support has been linked to depression, loneliness, and isolation, and has been shown to alter brain function and increase the risk of the following:

- Alcohol use
- Cardiovascular disease
- Depression
- Suicide

BREAKDOWN OF INTIMATE RELATIONSHIPS

First Responders are some of the bravest individuals in our communities, risking their lives daily to protect and serve. But with such a demanding and high-stress job, their intimate relationships can suffer.

Studies have shown that divorce rates among First Responders are significantly higher than the national average—up to 60-75% according to research from the First Responder's Initiative.[77] This is due to the long hours, night shifts, and work on holidays that disrupt family dynamics and make it difficult for First Responders to spend quality time with their loved ones. And when they do come home, they may be hesitant to share details about their work due to confidentiality or not wanting to burden their spouse with Vicarious Trauma.

This lack of communication combined with compartmentalization can lead to trust issues and strain on the relationship.

While many First Responders are able to maintain successful relationships, it's important for them to establish open communication, provide mutual support, and seek help when needed to maintain them. If this relationship breaks down or ends in divorce, it can have a serious impact on a First Responder's well-being and emotional stability.

Intimate relationships are the closest and cut the deepest. They're like the front lines in a First Responder's social support network.

Divorce can be an incredibly difficult and emotional experience for anyone. But for First Responders, who already face high levels of stress and trauma in their line of work, it can have an even more devastating impact on their mental well-being. Not only do they lose a partner, but often the breakdown of a family unit means losing children as well.

And it's not just about losing loved ones. Divorce can also sever important social support networks, including in-laws and mutual friends.

Without the support of a partner, family, or close friends, First Responders may find themselves feeling isolated and struggling to cope.

When social support systems are chipped away, so too is that protection against symptoms of depression, PTSD, anxiety, and other psychiatric disorders.

In situations like these, it's crucial to have access to peer support groups or group therapy to connect with others who understand the unique challenges divorce presents.

By seeking this kind of support, First Responders can find solace in knowing they are not alone and receive valuable advice from those who have walked in their shoes.

RETIREMENT AND SEPARATION FROM PEER SUPPORT

You might be thinking 50 years old or older when I say retirement. However, for professions like First Responders, early retirement due to unforeseen circumstances is common.

But retirement for these individuals can be a difficult transition, as their work has been a major source of purpose and identity.

First Responders, whether police officers, firefighters, or EMS professionals, chose their careers to serve and help others in their communities. And with that comes a unique bond among peers who understand the daily struggles and crises they face on the job.

But when retirement comes, this connection is lost and many First Responders find themselves feeling isolated from the world they once belonged to.

This isolation can also trigger a loss of identity, as these individuals are used to following strict protocols and being part of a structured environment.

Suddenly having all the time and freedom in the world can be overwhelming and bring up memories from their time on the job.

Apart from the loss of purpose, one of the biggest reasons why retired First Responders experience mental health crises is unresolved trauma from their time on the job.

When they were on daily calls, debriefs at the end were

helpful for them, offering a chance to discuss situations and bring fears and concerns out to others who understood the mental and physical toll. But after retirement, First Responders often struggle to process their trauma without being able to speak with those who understand.

Retirees may be able to speak to family and friends about their experiences, their loved ones may struggle to understand their perspective and can get traumatized as well.

The consequences of this new loneliness—and isolation from their former work and friends—is profound, and can intensify the emotional weight they've already carried leading to a sense of hopelessness.

Untreated, this emotional turmoil can manifest in issues with physical health, too.

MENTAL HEALTH WARNING SIGNS FOR FIRST RESPONDERS

Burnout, hopelessness, and mental health issues like anxiety, depression, and PTSD are just some of the consequences of neglecting mental health in this profession.

And these struggles don't just stay within the workplace. They can also affect personal relationships, as the emotional toll of their job makes it difficult to connect with loved ones. This can lead to strained relationships and erode important support systems that help us cope with stress.

But beyond the individual level, neglected mental health among First Responders can also have serious consequences on their work performance.

Impaired judgement and decision-making abilities can jeopardize their safety and the safety of those they serve.

When mental health issues are ignored or left un-addressed, they can have alarming consequences.

If you or someone you know exhibits some or a combination of these signs, it may be time to seek help:

- Displaying out-of-control or reckless behaviors.
- Increasing feelings of anxiety or excessive worry.
- Hostility or insubordination towards others and supervisors.
- Withdrawing or isolating behaviors.
- Changes in sleeping patterns.
- An increased use, or beginning use of drugs or alcohol to cope.
- An unusual fascination with suicide or homicide.
- Threatening suicide or threatening harm to others.

CHAPTER 4 EMERGENCY SERVICE WORKERS COMMON EXPOSURE POINTS

Now that we know the various forms of trauma that affect First Responders, let's look at their common exposure points for each type of emergency service worker and the unique stigmas and barriers they face.

LAW ENFORCEMENT OFFICER (LEO)

LEOs are patrol, peace, police, and public safety officers whose primary responsibility is to protect lives and property, but they often play a role in providing emotional support to community members in need. They may offer comfort and information to victims of crime or natural disasters, serving as a beacon of stability in chaotic and traumatic situations.

LEOs are expected to maintain peace and order, show compassion toward victims, and save those who are in danger. From the very beginning of their training, LEOs are taught the importance of dedication, integrity, and self-sacrifice in fulfilling these duties. However, this can also lead to what is known as a savior complex, or white knight syndrome, where LEOs feel pressure to respond to every emergency call and save everyone in need.[78]

Unfortunately, due to circumstances beyond their control, they may not always be able to protect or support victims or apprehend dangerous criminals. In such situations, LEOs may experience **Moral Distress**.[79]

Researchers have suggested that this Moral Distress among professionals in caregiving roles can ultimately result in **Compassion Fatigue** among LEOs.[80]

LEOs have a strong desire to help and protect victims of trauma while being limited in their ability to do so. Compassion Fatigue due to prolonged exposure to traumatized individuals can lead to difficulties emotionally disengaging from the suffering of others. This can hinder decision-making abilities in critical situations and negatively impact the well-being of the LEO, causing them to become numb, avoid critical incidents, and even consider resignation from their job.[81]

Of course, an LEO's work involves more than just caring for others. LEOs are also exposed to dangerous situations and gruesome crimes including hostage situations, drug busts, responding to fatal accidents, and handling cases involving serious injury or death.

> **Police Complex Spiral Trauma** (PCST) is the term used to describe the impact of **Cumulative Trauma** experienced by LEOs during their career.

Other factors can compound an LEO's stress load, such as long hours, dealing with difficult people, constantly being on call, uncertainty about what they will encounter next, and politics within the department. On top of all that, LEOs often face criticism and scrutiny for their actions.

It is possible that Cumulative Trauma, experienced over time, could impair an LEO's ability to perform their duties, make sound decisions, or control their negative emotions.[82]

Those working in law enforcement, no matter what capacity, will face difficult situations and routinely encounter criminal and violent acts as part of their jobs. In their line of duty, LEOs may have to use lethal force. Killing someone during a use of force encounter is considered the most stressful experience for officers.[83] If LEOs make a mistake that results in the death of a colleague, or were forced to follow orders that go against their personal beliefs, the situation goes beyond **Moral Distress** and lead to **Moral Injury**.[84]

Moral Injury is an intense kind of suffering that causes a person to lose their sense of being a good person.

Moral Injury can contribute to distress among LEOs similar to what soldiers experience on the battlefield. They wonder who they have become or think that who they have become is so awful they no longer deserve love or compassion. An individual may also lose perception of the world as a safe place and other human beings as individuals they can trust as a result.

It's intensely painful. Moral Injury is a deep suffering because in a high stakes situation. Something went wrong and either the LEO couldn't prevent it or were forced to cause harm to another human being. LEOs who are more spiritual are also more likely to experience distress, possibly due to the clash between their religious beliefs (e.g., "Thou shall not kill") and their actions in the line of duty.

LEOs who have killed or severely injured a perpetrator
are at higher risk of developing PTSD
if they do not address their Moral Injury.[85]

According to the National Center for Injury Prevention and Control, CDC, people in high-stress jobs, like First Responders are more prone to self-medication and develop co-occurring Substance Use Disorders (SUDs) to relieve their stress.[86]

While dealing with the high-pressure nature of their jobs is a factor, First Responders may also turn to alcohol for other reasons like building camaraderie, receiving peer support, and winding down at the end of the day.

Many engage in social drinking without developing a dependence on alcohol, but for those who do develop SUDs, it can exacerbate underlying mental and physical health issues causing more problems with job performance, personal relationships, and overall well-being.[87]

Suicide is also a significant concern among LEOs, though it's not exclusively caused by exposure to traumatic events. Lack of social support is a major factor contributing to feelings of hopelessness and suicide among LEOs.[88]

FIREFIGHTERS

A firefighter (whether a volunteer or career) is a First Responder who specializes in controlling and extinguishing fires that pose a threat to life and property. Firefighters also have to be **Emergency Medical Technicians** (EMTs) as part of their job includes rescuing individuals from dangerous situations, giving first aid, and CPR.

Many firefighters expand their training to become paramedics as well. Beyond medical training, firefighters need the physical strength and stamina to help people in emergencies. They work closely with other emergency response agencies, like the police and medical services, which is why their job overlaps with these other roles.

Among emergency workers, firefighters are especially vulnerable due to experiencing negative mental health impacts throughout their career.[89]

The unpredictable and intense nature of their job can cause significant stressors both on and off-duty. Their schedules often involve long shifts followed by a limited amount of time off, causing disruption to their sleep patterns. This can lead to sleep disturbances, which is another occupational hazard.

Additionally, being away from family or working opposite shifts from a spouse can add to the existing stressors for firefighters. Missing important family moments like milestones or events can take a heavy toll on their mental well-being.[90]

A recent *What Firefighters Want* survey asked more than 2100 firefighters about their stress. On a scale of 1-10, approximately 76% of firefighters rated their stress level between 6 and 10, with 8 being the most common answer.

- 47% stated that stress from the job is negatively impacting relationships with family.

- 50% stated that stress is negatively impacting their ability to engage in hobbies, vacations, etc.
- 67% state that stress levels are negatively impacting their ability to sleep, time to exercise, etc.
- 42% of respondents stated that their stress level has caused them to consider leaving the fire service.[91]

Despite choosing this profession out of a passion for helping others and saving lives, constantly being exposed to death, injury, and suffering can come at a cost.

The cumulative stressors of physical strain, long hours, work-related sleep issues, and difficulty balancing work and home life can lead to symptoms like anxiety, irritability, nervousness, and problems with memory and concentration. Over time, this chronic stress can contribute to the development of anxiety and depression, with lasting effects on the brain. In fact, a 2014 report from the *National Fallen Firefighters Foundation* found that a fire department is three times more likely to experience a suicide in a given year than a line-of-duty death.[92]

Among women in the US, the occupations with the highest suicide rates are police and firefighters, with a rate of 14.1 per 100 000.[93] According to the National Center for Injury Prevention and Control (NCIPC), mental stress of the job can lead to substance abuse and alcohol abuse as ways of coping with the stress.[94]

Where there's a trauma or tragedy, firefighters are often the first on the scene. Firefighters are exposed to potentially traumatic situations by the nature of their work. On any given day, they may encounter house fires, car accidents, terrorist attacks, and other emergency situations. **Repeated exposure trauma**, the severity of the incidents that firefighters are involved in, and the emotional skills needed to cope with **Cumulative Trauma** can lead to **Compassion Fatigue, Secondary Traumatic Stress, Vicarious Trauma, Burnout, and PTSD.**[95]

Every individual's experience and risk for developing PTSD is unique. Some may go through years of service before displaying symptoms while others may develop them after just one incident.

However, firefighters with traits such as high hostility, low self-esteem, neuroticism, past trauma, and limited social support face a higher risk of developing PTSD.[96]

First Responders across all positions have a higher rate of alcohol consumption, including heavy and binge drinking, compared to the general population. [97]

According to the NCIPC, people in high-stress jobs, like First Responders are more prone to self-medication and can develop co-occurring SUDs to relieve their stress.[98]

While dealing with the high-pressure nature of their jobs is a factor, First Responders may also turn to alcohol for other reasons like building camaraderie, receiving peer support, and winding down at the end of the day.

Many engage in social drinking without developing a dependence on alcohol, but for those who do develop SUDs, it can exacerbate underlying mental and physical health issues causing more problems with job performance, personal relationships, and overall well-being.[99]

Suicide is also a significant concern among firefighters, though it's not exclusively caused by exposure to traumatic events. Lack of social support is a major factor contributing to feelings of hopelessness and suicide among First Responders.[100]

VOLUNTEER EMERGENCY SERVICE WORKERS (ESWS)

One major distinction between firefighters and their mental health is whether they are serving in career versus volunteer departments.

While most research has focused on the mental health of paid career Emergency Service Workers (ESWs), the reality is that the majority of firefighters in Western countries are actually volunteers. In the United States alone, 67% of firefighters are volunteers while only 33% are career firefighters.[101] Though some may serve in both paid and volunteer positions, it's important to recognize the distinct differences between these two groups.

Although volunteer firefighters do not receive a salary for their service, they may be reimbursed for expenses such as food, transportation, and supplies. They may also receive certain benefits, including life insurance and health insurance, which equal about 20% of what a career firefighter earns.[102]

The nature of firefighting, whether voluntary or professional, exposes individuals to high levels of occupational stress and repeated traumatic events. On any given day, they may encounter house fires, car accidents, terrorist attacks, and other emergency situations. Repeated exposure to trauma, the severity of the incidents that firefighters are involved in, and the emotional skills needed to cope with **Cumulative Trauma** can lead to **Compassion Fatigue, Secondary Traumatic Stress, Vicarious Trauma, and Burnout**.

Studies have shown that volunteer firefighters often experience higher levels of PTSD symptoms compared to paid career rescue workers after major traumatic events.[103] Additionally, volunteers have higher rates of depression, suicidal thoughts, and attempted suicide than paid career firefighters.[104]

This could be due to the lack of pre-employment psychological screenings, heightened work/family conflict caused by the demands of their volunteer role, limited training on mental health and critical incidents, and potential challenges in accessing mental health care.[105]

Volunteer departments often have fewer resources available for their members.

The National Volunteer Fire Council (NVFC) has a program called "Share the Load" which provides a database of licensed mental health professionals.[106] Through this program, firefighters and their families can learn about suicide and other mental health issues through various courses, newsletters, and videos. The NVFC also offers multiple ways to access the Suicide Prevention Lifeline, including by phone, online chat, or text.

Additionally, the International Association of Fire Fighters (IAFF) has a trained peer support network composed of fellow firefighters who understand mental health concerns and can connect members (mostly career firefighters) with community resources and mental health professionals if needed. [107]

SEARCH AND RESCUE (SAR)

Search and Rescue (SAR) is the process of looking for and offering assistance to individuals in danger or distress.

It encompasses various specialized fields, each tailored to different types of terrain.

These include:

- Mountain rescue
- Ground search and rescue with the help of K9 units
- Urban search and rescue in cities
- Combat search and rescue on the battlefield
- Air-sea rescue over water

SAR personnel are routinely exposed to difficult situations as they put their own lives at risk to help others. They conduct searches in challenging environments, regardless of weather conditions or time of day or year.

The specific type of SAR responder called upon depends on the required expertise for the particular terrain.

SAR work can be hazardous and volunteers often receive no compensation or healthcare benefits, despite the potential physical injuries and mental health impacts from witnessing traumatic events or death.

In the United States, there are multiple organizations responsible for SAR at national, state, and local levels.

Most daily SAR operations in the US are led by County Sheriffs, although some states such as Alaska have State Highway Patrol overseeing SAR efforts. In certain areas, local fire departments, EMS services, or non-profit agencies may also provide SAR assistance.

Members of SAR teams typically receive training in Incident Command System (ICS), first aid, and necessary outdoor skills for their designated terrain and climate.

Though search and rescue teams receive important training to help them perform their duties, there are very few full-time SAR roles or opportunities for individuals to pursue.

Most often, aspiring SAR professionals work other, relevant full-time jobs on the side and stay on call for any potential search and rescue situations.

The most common career fields that offer search and rescue opportunities include:

- Law enforcement
- National parks employees
- Firefighters
- Emergency organizations
- United States military

Like other First Responders, SAR personnel are frequently exposed to traumatic incidents in their line of duty. This includes life-threatening situations, severe injuries, and the loss of colleagues and civilians. As a result, they face a higher risk of developing **Compassion Fatigue**, **Acute Stress Disorder (ASD)**, and PTSD.

As with volunteer firefighters, SAR personnel have higher rates of depression, suicidal thoughts, and attempted suicide than paid career First Responders.[108] This could be due to the heightened work/family conflict caused by the demands of their work, limited training on mental health care and critical incidents, and challenges accessing care.[109]

Over the years, the demands placed on SAR personnel have become more challenging as outdoor recreation grows in popularity without an equivalent increase in volunteer-based rescue services available.[110]

> While it may seem glamorous, SAR work is far from it.
> There are no set hours and teams must be prepared to spend
> the night in the field if necessary.

SAR teams undergo rigorous training and live their lives on-call, ready to help others at a moment's notice.

SAR personnel are often faced with the reality that it will take hours and sometimes days to reach those who need rescuing. Some of the people that are rescued will be beyond help when they are found. And those who are found but require medical treatment will have the added insult of prolonged suffering and exposure to the elements as they are transported to a care facility.

SAR personnel are required to handle themselves and the operation in a professional manner while dealing directly with people's suffering. Unfortunately, **Burnout** and **high levels of stress** among SAR personnel are common and their risk of PTSD is comparable to other First Responder groups.[111]

EMERGENCY MEDICAL SERVICES PERSONNEL

EMS is composed of various job positions and individuals who are the first to respond in times of crisis.

Emergency Medical Dispatchers (EMDs) are trained to respond to 911 calls and can provide vital instructions over the phone to those reporting medical emergencies, guiding them through critical situations such as blocked airways, bleeding, childbirth, and cardiac arrest.

Emergency Medical Technicians (EMTs) are trained to respond to 911 calls and other life-threatening situations, providing immediate care and transporting patients to hospitals.

Paramedics have gone through more extensive training than EMTs and are qualified to perform advanced procedures and offer advanced life support.

Many jurisdictions require firefighters to obtain certification as an EMT or paramedic.

Emergency Room (ER) Techs are paramedics working in hospitals providing medical services in the emergency room department similar to nurses.

Registered Nurses (RNs) and **Emergency Room (ER) Doctors** work in hospitals providing medical services in the emergency room department.

The job of an EMS provider is inherently stressful, involving constant exposure to human suffering and trauma.

Shifts as an EMS provider can vary drastically in terms of call volume, and providers are often working outside in harsh weather conditions at all hours of the day. Emergencies can occur anywhere, from public locations like streets and shopping centers to intimate settings like private residences or nursing homes. Additionally, EMS providers may encounter violent or traumatic situations while on the job, making their work even more challenging. Repeated exposure to trauma, the severity of the incidents that EMS providers are involved in, and the emotional skills needed to cope with **Cumulative Trauma** can lead to **Compassion Fatigue**, **Secondary Traumatic**

Stress, **Vicarious Trauma**, and **Burnout**.

Every individual's experience and risk for developing PTSD is unique; some may go through years of service before displaying symptoms while others may have an immediate impact.

> The top three stressors universally associated with poor mental health include career challenges, financial struggles, and lack of sleep.[112]

A study from 2018 found that Paramedics have the highest rate of PTSD.[113] This is likely due to the top three stressors universally associated with poor mental health including career challenges, financial struggles, and lack of sleep.

Shift lengths and rotations vary depending on each EMS agency's policies. Working irregular schedules disrupts providers' natural sleep patterns and can lead to exhaustion. Many providers also work overtime or hold multiple jobs to make ends meet, resulting in back-to-back shifts and further fatigue.

Considering the long shifts, standard pay rates, and exposure to traumatic events, it's not surprising that EMS providers are considered high-risk for developing mental health issues.[114]

While lack of sleep and financial concerns are common issues for EMS providers, the nature of their occupation is the biggest contributor to an increased risk of mental health issues.

With the increase of disasters around the world, the demand for EMS providers is higher than ever as they play a crucial role in disaster management systems; however, an estimated 69% of EMS providers report not having enough recovery time between traumatic incidents.[115] Most EMS providers are expected to be on duty for strenuous amounts of time—up to and beyond 24 hours. The duration and intensity of being on-call, engaging in extremely stressful situations, and having little opportunity for rest in between incidents can lead to Burnout.

EMS providers, who work in high-risk environments and make life-or-death decisions on a regular basis, are particularly vulnerable to Burnout.[116] A study of retired EMS providers found that 92% experienced some level of Burnout during their career.

Burnout can result in medical errors that harm patients and greatly impact the quality of life for EMS professionals.[117]

Although EMTs and paramedics are often the first responders, they are not the only ones in the EMS chain suffering from Burnout. Reports show that other EMS personnel are also experiencing increasing levels of Burnout within the industry. Nurses have reported feelings of emotional exhaustion and depersonalization—two key components of Burnout.

The job of an Emergency Dispatcher may not require them to physically enter a scene, but they still face daily challenges and trauma that can take a toll on their mental health. Emergency Dispatchers act as the vital link between individuals in crisis and First Responders, responsible for dispatching assistance to both emergency and non-emergency situations. They must remain level-headed and composed while handling multiple tasks and finding solutions on-the-spot amidst dangerous and heartbreaking situations such as home invasions, domestic violence incidents, fires, car accidents, and even murders.

According to recent findings from the *Pulse of 9-1-1 State of the Industry Survey*, 74% of respondents reported staff Burnout at their 9-1-1 centers, with many displaying symptoms of anxiety, fatigue, and low energy levels. Despite over 90% of employers offering wellness support services, only 18% of respondents actually utilize them.[118]

These results align with a 2021 survey conducted by Pew Charitable Trusts in 27 states, which found that most responding 911 call centers do not provide behavioral health crisis training for their employees.[119]

Moral Distress is a major factor that contributes to mental health issues among EMS providers.

EMS providers must respect a person's choice to refuse medical assistance, even if it may result in their death. In fact, a study revealed that 27% of ethical conflicts during paramedic responses were due to issues with informed consent or refusal.[120] EMS workers feel a sense of duty to respond and may struggle with moral responsibility to provide care, even if the patient denies treatment or transport—regardless of medical advice.[121 122]

The effects of Burnout, Moral Distress, and Cumulative Trauma are not limited to EMS providers. Feelings of powerlessness and decreased job satisfaction have been reported in all medical professions. [123 124]

To address mental health issues within EMS organizations, strategies such as focus groups, Critical Incident

Stress Management (CISM) programs, and Employee Assistance Programs (EAPs) have been implemented. These programs aim to provide personnel who have experienced traumatic events with guidance and support from coaches or counselors trained in grief management techniques and therapy options.[125]

EMS providers, like the other responders we have discussed, have a higher rate of alcohol consumption, including heavy and binge drinking, compared to the general population. While dealing with the stressful nature of their jobs is a factor, emergency response personnel may also turn to alcohol for social reasons.

While many First Responders engage in social drinking without developing a dependence on alcohol, for those who do, it can have devastating effects on both their personal and professional lives.[126]

CHAPTER 5 PTSD DOWN AND DIRTY FACTS

Not everyone who is exposed to trauma or traumatic events will develop symptoms of PTSD, but the possibility is there. That's where the criteria come into play. There are five major criteria to PTSD that we need to know about, because they are what our therapist will use to diagnose our PTSD.

> **Criteria** are the standards on which a diagnosis is decided. **Criteria** is plural; **criterion** is singular.

CRITERION A: DEFINITION

This criterion gives us the DSM's definition of trauma: "Actual or threatened exposure to death, serious injury, or sexual violence." This is a big umbrella; there are many life events that could fit under it. Chapter 3 outlined many of the traumas that fall under this umbrella.

As you're probably already noticing, trauma is a ubiquitous experience, especially for First Responders.

Let's talk about the term *"Actual or threatened exposure."* We all have a physical and psychological reaction to threats: fight, flight, freeze, or tend-and-befriend (which is more common among women.)

Our body and brain will react the same whether the threat is *actual* or *threatened*.

Our brain's #1 job is to keep us alive. When there is a perceived threat, our hearts beat faster to get more blood to our muscles, our eyes dilate, and we sweat or shake. This is our brain preparing us to do what we need to in order to stay alive.

Easy day. Now that we know what the trauma response is, we go to...

CRITERION B: INTRUSION SYMPTOMS

Let's say an intruder breaks into our home. They break in when we're not ready or expecting it and they try to take all our stuff. That's what intrusion symptoms feel like.

We're going to go through these five intrusion symptoms and translate again from clinician-to-English so that we've got this.

Intrusion Symptom 1 *as written*:
"Recurrent, involuntary, and intrusive distressing memories of the traumatic event(s)."

Translation:
"We can't stop thinking about it."

Intruders come into our house when we don't want them, and we have zero control over them. This is what intrusive memories do.

They break into our mind when we don't want them to, they do what they want, and it happens a lot (our brain is in a bad neighborhood).

Intrusion Symptom 2 as written:
"Recurrent, distressing dreams in which the content and/or affect of the dream are related to the traumatic event(s)."

Translation:
"Nightmares… weird dreams that can feel scary."

Recurrent means that they happen over and over, and distressing means that they're stressful.

On TV, when someone has a nightmare or a flashback, they relive the trauma happening again exactly the way it did originally in real life. But nightmares can be uniquely terrifying in ways all their own.

They can have elements of our trauma, elements of our fears, and other powerful emotions.

Intrusion Symptom 3 as written:
"Dissociative reactions (e.g. flashbacks) in which the individual feels or acts as if the traumatic event(s) were occurring."

Translation:
 "Strange feelings/experiences that remind us of the trauma, mess with our head, and make us feel crazy."

Dissociation is a 50-cent word that means *disconnection*, and PTSD can definitely make us feel disconnected from ourselves.

Sometimes, this looks like intense emotions that come out of nowhere, and we feel sad or anxious "for no reason."

Sometimes, it feels like everything around us isn't real or is "off" and we can't really explain it.

Sometimes, it looks more like confusion. Unfortunately, this is normal for PTSD.

Since this topic is already uncomfortable, let's go a little deeper in the water: *Hallucinations*. This is when we see, hear, smell, taste, or feel something we objectively know is not there.

Like when we smell something burning (and we know there's no fire) or we hear gunshots, or think we see people following us.

Straight facts, from a clinician viewpoint.

I have very rarely seen cases of PTSD without hallucinations.

And we need to talk about this openly because hallucinations make us feel legit crazy in a way that other symptoms don't. Ditto for flashbacks.

WHAT'S A FLASHBACK?

Like nightmares, flashbacks are nothing like we see in the movies. Flashbacks can feel like walking talking nightmares. They are intense episodes that happen while we're fully awake. Flashbacks strike suddenly and feel uncontrollable. They are more like a nightmare than a memory because sometimes we can't tell the difference between a flashback and reality. They're vivid and feel unbelievably real. Unlike a movie clip, in flashbacks we can vividly see, hear, taste, and smell things. It's terrifying because it feels like the trauma is happening all over again. Those of us who experience flashbacks often feel like we're going insane. We're not. This is a known PTSD symptom.

When we don't know that hallucinations and flashbacks are an expected part of PTSD, we can feel like we're going crazy and have no way of stopping the visions from haunting us. This leads many to seriously consider suicide.

When experiencing recurring hallucinations and flashbacks, we stop trusting our brain and body. We become frightened of ourselves and our reactions.

We may ask ourselves, *"What if I hurt my family?"* or *"What if I lose it in the middle of Walmart?"*

When we use this logic, suicide makes a lot of sense (but it isn't the answer). We very much get you; it can feel like we'll never come back from this. **But we can.**

For now, let this sink in:

Hallucinations and flashbacks are a normal part of PTSD.

Normal doesn't mean that it's okay. It just means that hallucinations and flashbacks are common and not unexpected. This is par for the course. **You are not a freak.**

Symptoms 4 and 5 are two sides of the same coin, so we'll group them together.

Intrusion Symptom 4&5 as written:
"Intense or prolonged psychological distress (symptom 4) or physical distress (symptom 5) to internal or external cues."

Translation:
"Triggers mess with our physical bodies and our minds."

We all have physical and psychological reactions to threats. This means that our bodies and our brains react. *Cues* are better described as **triggers**.

Triggers: Stimuli that cause our bodies and brains to react.

Triggers can be internal (like pain) or external (like the sound of a car backfiring). They can bring us right back to our trauma. The smell of our attacker's cologne, a box in the middle of the road, the sound of a gunshot - these are all examples of potential triggers.

Triggers can make our hearts race and/or cause a full-blown panic attack. Unfortunately, we don't know our triggers until we experience them. It's the worst kind of surprise.

FOOT STOMP

For criterion B, the DSM-5 states that we must have one or more of these symptoms. So, if we meet one out of five, or we won the PTSD lottery and have them all, we meet this criterion. This is a common clinical error; we do not have to have all five symptoms to meet this criterion.

CRITERION C: AVOIDANCE SYMPTOMS

The DSM defines this as avoiding *internal things* (like memories, thoughts, or feelings) or avoiding *external things* (like people, places, and things that remind us of the trauma).

Those of us with PTSD will go way out of our way to avoid anything that reminds us of our trauma.

Thank you, Captain Obvious!

This makes a lot of sense. **Why *wouldn't* we want to dodge memories and reactions that make us feel crazy?** This is why drug and alcohol disorders are common with PTSD: numbing the pain is easier.

Friends, we'll go way, way out of our way to avoid anything that reminds us of our trauma.

While this may seem downright insane to other people, it makes total sense in the context of PTSD.

Common examples are:

- Stop watching the news or using social media because of stories or posts that remind us of a trauma.
- Go out of our way to stay away from the scene of our attack or places that remind us of the assault.
- Running errands at odd hours to avoid crowds.
- Arriving early so we can choose a seat away from the window.

Avoidance can get complex; we will go to extremes to avoid potential triggers. Our brain's job is (1) to keep us alive, and (2) to understand meaning. Avoidance is incredibly logical in this context, so be easy on yourself.

CRITERION D: "NEGATIVE ALTERATION IN COGNITION AND MOOD."

This means "negative changes in our thoughts and feelings." There are seven of these symptoms, and we need *two out of seven* to meet this criterion. Let's go through them.

Symptom 1: We can't remember important parts of the trauma.

When our bodies are in fight, flight, or freeze response, our brains shift everything to survival. It's not unusual for folks with PTSD to forget or not remember significant aspects of the trauma until a trigger strikes.

Symptom 2: Persistent and exaggerated negative beliefs about ourselves, other people, and the world.

In Cognitive Processing Therapy, we call these "stuck points," and they definitely get us stuck. We start to believe extreme thoughts, like:

People wouldn't die if I was better at my job.

I have to control everything on each call.

Expressing emotion is a loss of control.

Symptom 3: Persistent and distorted thoughts about what caused the trauma or what happened because of the trauma.

These thoughts lead us to blame ourselves or others. Self-blame is common, even when we know our thoughts are not logical. These are thoughts like:

I don't deserve to live because I let other people die.

If I can't protect people, what good am I?

If I didn't freeze, I could have done something differently.

These distorted thoughts feel 100% convincing, but we need to ask ourselves if it's possible that we're wrong. We don't have to decide one way or the other, but we need to ask if it's *possible*.

The reason we need to talk about this is that these thoughts make us want to commit suicide. More on this later, but for now, let's leave this here:

If it's possible that we're wrong, then it's possible killing ourselves isn't the right answer.

TRUTH BOMB: LET'S TALK ABOUT FREEZING

We hear about fight or flight all the time, but freeze is the red-headed stepchild of trauma. All three, fight, flight, _and_ freeze, are all normal neuro-biological responses to fear, but, if we don't know this, we can feel guilty, angry, or like we "let it happen" when our body freezes in the face of trauma.

First, let's address the fantasy that we have a choice whether our body goes into fight, flight, or freeze, because that's not a thing. When we're in danger, our brain kicks into high gear and takes over to protect our life. We do not get a choice; in a split second our brain makes the choice for us.

Think about those nature shows where lions are hunting gazelle-snacks. Flight or freeze are legit survival methods.

Symptom 4: Persistent negative emotional state (e.g., fear, horror, anger, guilt, or shame).

We feel crappy - a lot.

Symptom 5: Diminished interest or participation in significant activities.

Relaxing and having fun can feel like a colossal waste of time. It's easier to stay at home. Even things we used to enjoy don't meet the muster anymore: going out with friends, relaxing, reading, or taking a bath.

This can affect our family, too, because we're not spending as much time with them.

We only have so much bandwidth, friend.

When our mind is busy combatting all those intrusion symptoms and avoiding things, it's hard to concentrate on anything else, especially relaxing or having fun.

Symptom 6: Feeling detached or estranged from others.

Feeling disconnected and alienated from other people is common.

Symptom 7: Persistent inability to feel positive emotions.

This one is going to hurt - but if we can't talk about it here, where can we?

Let's think of emotions as a continuum: on one side we have all our bad emotions that we don't want to feel, like sadness, guilt, or loss.

In the middle are medium feelings like "meh," ambivalence, or not caring, and on the other end are good emotions we want to feel, like happiness, joy, and laughter. It looks like this:

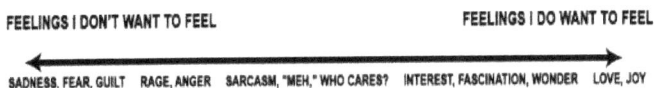

FEELINGS I DON'T WANT TO FEEL   FEELINGS I DO WANT TO FEEL

◄─────────────────────────────────────►

SADNESS, FEAR, GUILT   RAGE, ANGER   SARCASM, "MEH," WHO CARES?   INTEREST, FASCINATION, WONDER   LOVE, JOY

Remember criterion C, avoidance? That's when we go way out of our way to avoid anything that reminds us of our trauma. This includes all the stuff we don't want to feel, like regret and sorrow. It makes sense that we want to avoid feeling crappy, and the hope is that we can avoid feeling crappy and enjoy the right side of the scale only. That makes sense, but feelings don't work that way.

See, things on this feelings continuum attenuate from both ends in equal measure. This means that when we avoid those crappy feelings on the left, we become *unable* to feel the good feelings we want on the right. It's a completely unexpected second-order effect, but that's how the brain works. We avoid the feelings on the left and the feelings from the right reduce in equal measure until our continuum looks like this:

FEELINGS I DON'T WANT TO FEEL   FEELINGS I DO WANT TO FEEL

NUMB

We've worked to avoid the things we don't want to feel, but now we literally cannot feel joy, laughter, or happiness.

We end up in this horrible place called "numb" and it feels frightening.

Our spouse will come up to us and want to discuss something deeply upsetting - and we know they have every right to be upset - but we feel nothing.

Our friends will try to talk to us about how we've been acting, and we can see they are worried about us, but it feels like we're outside of ourselves watching this whole interaction.

Our kids come up to us crying, and we don't feel anything. Maybe we even think, "quit your crying, you big baby." *Did I just really think that?*

We feel nothing, and we know we should feel something.

We can ask ourselves, *"What is wrong with me? What kind of monster feels nothing?"* or think, *"Maybe I really am an animal."* We google our questions to see if we're a psychopath. (Calm down; you're not a psychopath.)

After feeling numb for a while, we get an idea: *I'll kill myself.* Suddenly, unexpectedly, we feel *something*. It's not joy, but it's not numb. In fact, it's the first time we've felt something outside of numb for a while - the closest we've been to feeling happy in a long time. Not because suicide ever fixes things the way we think it will, but because we have an answer when we didn't have one before. Any feelings at this point are amazing. It's at this point that we tell ourselves the lie,

"This must be the best way - because why would I feel this way if it wasn't?"

This is amplified by outside validation from people who care about us—our spouse, colleagues, and friends. They say, *"It's good to see you smiling again! You look like you're doing better today!"*

They are happy to see us feeling something again. We are happy to be feeling anything at all, and it is all because of the lie. That only reinforces it in our minds. We think it has to be the solution.

Fast forward: it's not.

FEELINGS ARE NOT FACTS.

We're going to have some real talk about suicide in a future chapter because no one talks about it and we need to. We're not trying to read you.

We've experienced this and heard this echoed thousands of times with clients.

If you're feeling this way right now, put this book down and read **Suicide: The Forever Decision** by Paul G. Quinnett, PhD. It's available in several places to download the PDF for free. Dr. Quinnett is brilliant, and we highly recommend it.

Remember: We only need 2/7 symptoms to meet this criterion.

We know this is exhausting. Last one:

CRITERION E: SIGNIFICANT CHANGES IN AROUSAL OR REACTIVITY ASSOCIATED WITH THE TRAUMA

This kind of arousal doesn't have to do with sex. In this case, arousal means that your brain and your body are alert, awake, and ready. This makes sense because:

If our brain doesn't feel safe, it will keep us on high alert so we don't get hurt

---

Pure logic from our brain's perspective, but this doesn't work well in everyday life. Like criterion D, **this requires two symptoms**, not all of them.

Symptom 1: Irritable Behavior or Angry Outbursts (with little or no provocation) - can be verbal or physical

You've been through some stuff. This happens.

Symptom 2: Reckless or Self-Destructive Behavior

High-risk behavior on PTSD is a different animal. Think of driving your motorcycle without a helmet, while high, to pick up your daughter from daycare (true case). Think back to avoidance, too - we destroy our good marriages, eviscerate our best friends, and show up drunk to family reunions. Total self-destruction - now you know why.

Symptom 3: Hypervigilance

This is heightened alertness and behavior aimed at keeping us safe. We stay on guard, even when we logically know we're okay. Our brain and body stay alert and ready for fight, flight, or freeze. It's exhausting to maintain this for a prolonged period, and we can't relax.

Symptom 4: Exaggerated Startle Response

Being startled (shocked, surprised) is an unconscious defensive response to sudden noises or perceived threats. We always feel on edge.

Symptom 5: Problems with Concentration

We only have so much bandwidth, so when our mind is busy with intrusion symptoms and avoidance, it's hard to concentrate on anything else.

Symptom 6: Problems Sleeping

These can be problems falling asleep, staying asleep, or experiencing restless sleep.

Remember: We only need 2/6 symptoms to meet this criterion.

We'll cover the last three criteria in brief because they are not complicated.

Criterion F says that these symptoms have been around for over one month.

Criterion G wants to ensure that these symptoms are problematic and are affecting our everyday real life.

Criterion H reminds us that if these symptoms are the result of a substance (like a medication) or a physical illness, then it's not PTSD.

C-PTSD

While we are talking about PTSD, we also need to address Complex PTSD (C-PTSD). The two are similar in their root causes, with the C- distinction reflecting the complexity of issues that develop due to the repetitive nature of the trauma experienced over a long period of time.

> The distinction between PTSD and C-PTSD is important because many of the traumas we will outline in this book are ones that happen over long periods of time, and that alters the presentation and recovery treatments needed to heal.

The current edition of the *Diagnostic and Statistical Manual of Mental Disorders* (DSM-5) does not separate PTSD from C-PTSD, however, the World Health Organization (WHO) does include C-PTSD as its own separate diagnosis (6B41) in the 11th revision of the *International Statistical Classification of Diseases and Related Health Problems* (ICD-11).[127]

Because the diagnosis of C-PTSD is not included in the DSM-5 and the cluster of symptoms that present with this distinctive diagnosis often overlaps with other mood disorders, it can be difficult for clinicians to identify. Many individuals who should be diagnosed with C-PTSD downplay their trauma and have developed unique coping mechanisms, which, more often than not, are failing by the time they are seeking help. This makes them appear as high-functioning people, further confusing the diagnosis.

SYMPTOMS OF COMPLEX PTSD

C-PTSD has many of the same symptoms as PTSD, including intrusive memories or flashbacks, depression, anxiety, avoidance, and changes in personality. However, people with C-PTSD also experience:

- **Loss of Systems of Meaning**
  Losing core values, religion, beliefs, or faith can cause a sense of hopelessness and despair.
- **Negative Self-Perception**
  Experiencing helplessness, shame, guilt, and self-loathing, while often expressing feelings of inadequacy or being different from others.
- **Changes in Consciousness**
  A person may have periods of amnesia (forgetting) or dissociation, making them feel detached from themselves or their surroundings.
- **Emotional Dysregulation**
  Difficulty in Controlling Emotions and/or Emotional flashbacks rather than intrusively remembering the traumatic event, a person with C-PTSD might instead become emotionally overwhelmed during periods of stress causing them to re-experience the emotions they felt during their trauma. This happens without recalling or thinking about the traumatic event.[128]

This distinction between PTSD and C-PTSD is important because a First Responder's job puts them in direct contact with trauma on a daily basis. Long-term exposure to trauma often necessitates an altered and sometimes longer approach to treatment.

While C-PTSD can be a severe and debilitating disorder, C-PTSD treatments do exist and are effective. Recovery from C-PTSD is a long process that often involves the standard treatments for PTSD (cognitive processing of the trauma), as well as additional psychotherapy to work with assistance for emotional regulation, skill building to overcome learned behaviors and habits that formed during the duration of the trauma, and somatic psychotherapy to help retrain the nervous system to function and respond appropriately instead of defaulting to stress responses.

This is especially important if the trauma experienced began during childhood.

SUBSTANCE ABUSE DISORDERS

According to the National Center for Injury Prevention and Control, CDC, people in high-stress jobs, like First Responders and healthcare workers, are more prone to engage in self-medicating.[129]

The constant pressure and exposure to traumatic events can lead to Cumulative Trauma and mental health issues like Acute Stress Disorder (ASD), depression, and post-traumatic stress disorder (PTSD).

Unfortunately, many individuals in these professions also develop co-occurring Substance Use Disorders (SUDs) to relieve their symptoms.

Self-medicating is a term used to describe individuals who turn to drugs or alcohol to cope with overwhelming emotions and feelings that they are not ready or able to confront.

This can take various forms, such as excessive use of alcohol, tobacco, or painkillers.

Drug and alcohol abuse make sense in the context of PTSD. Criterion C of PTSD is avoidance and drinking and drugging help us avoid our feelings. Criterion D is all about changes in the way we think and feel, and alcohol and drugs can play a major role in this.

While dealing with job stress is a contributing factor in SUDs, those in caregiving professions may also turn to alcohol for other reasons. Sometimes, a cold beer (or a few) at the end of a tough day eases the tension. Social drinking is good for bonding with your peers. You've been through hell with your brothers and sisters, and it would be a shame to miss some quality relaxation time with your team once the shift ends. A work culture where social drinking and bonding with peers is normal, but it's also an easy place for problems related to substance abuse to go unnoticed. For others, maybe they need to take the edge off of their physical pain from injury or muscle strain and they grab their bottle of painkillers. No one likes to be in pain, whether mental or physical, so numbing it is one answer—and an easy habit to fall into.

But what starts as a social norm or coping mechanism can quickly spiral into addiction. Many people don't even realize they have an SUD until they try to cut down or face negative consequences from their self-medicating.

Substance abuse symptoms can be physical, psychological, and behavioral.

Signs of substance abuse in First Responders include:

- Changes in behavior or mood swings
- Frequent absences from work or frequent tardiness
- Poor job performance or deterioration in work quality
- Financial problems or borrowing money frequently
- Unexplained injuries or accidents
- Secretive or suspicious behavior
- Neglecting personal hygiene or appearance
- Isolation from colleagues or friends
- Smelling of alcohol or drugs
- Sudden weight loss or gain

However, the good news is that SUDs are treatable. And peer support groups such as Alcoholics Anonymous or Narcotics Anonymous are vital parts of addiction treatment aftercare programs. They provide a safe and supportive environment during the recovery process and offer opportunities for individuals to discuss their successes, fears, and struggles while working towards sobriety.

The most successful peer support groups consist of people from a similar background. In the case of First Responders, finding a support group that consists of others in your field will not only provide an outlet to discuss and learn more about addiction but an outlet to communicate with peers about the day-to-day struggles that first led to addiction.

Check the resource section at the back of this book for a list of First Responder-specific mental health resources.

CHAPTER 6 BARRIERS TO HELP

STIGMAS

While First Responders are trained to deal with these extreme situations, they are often not equipped with resources for their mental health needs after the fact. It is expected that First Responders will encounter traumatic events, but many do not realize the long-term effects of repeated exposure on their mental well-being.[130]

First Responder culture strongly emphasizes strength, self-reliance, and saving others.[131]

One major reason that First Responders do not seek help for mental health issues is the societal expectation for them to always be the ones helping others. This mentality leads many First Responders to consider stress and trauma as just part of their job, making it difficult for them to admit when they are struggling and reach out for help. There is often a fear among First Responders that being honest about their mental health struggles could harm their career prospects.[132]

Sadly, fear of repercussion is partially legitimate.

Mental health is a requirement for being a First Responder, and people have, in fact, lost their weapons status or been remanded to "desk duty" after seeking out help for mental health challenges.

Fear of judgement can prevent First Responders from seeking help. In fact, one study found that officers who perceived their colleagues as judgmental were less likely to access mental health services themselves.[133]

The stigma surrounding mental health in the First Responder community also leads many individuals to underreport symptoms and avoid seeking help in order to avoid negative judgments or repercussions at work.

On average, about one third of First Responders experience stigma regarding mental health issues.[134]

PRACTICAL BARRIERS

Stigma is often the biggest obstacle that prevents First Responders from seeking mental health services. However, access to convenient services, cost, and compatibility with work schedules is a major factor too.

In an online survey of 525 firefighters throughout the United States, cost and availability were highlighted as major challenges when it came to accessing mental health services.

This is especially problematic for volunteer firefighters, who may face even more difficulty in obtaining the necessary support compared to career First Responders.[135]

Police officers, particularly those employed by smaller departments outside of urban areas, also encounter similar obstacles in accessing mental health services.[136]

LIMITED AVAILABILITY OF TRAUMA-COMPETENT MENTAL HEALTH RESOURCES

The limited availability of trauma–competent mental health resources specifically tailored towards First Responders is another hurdle. Oftentimes, general mental health practitioners, who may not be trauma-trained clinicians, are all that is available. Although they may be able to meet the needs of most clients, these practitioners may not possess the necessary knowledge or expertise to relate to First Responders or fully understand the complex nature of trauma experiences. If a First Responder finally does decide to seek treatment but encounters an unprepared provider, it can be extremely discouraging and potentially prevent them from seeking further help in the future. Therefore, it is crucial for First Responders have access to trauma-trained clinicians.[137]

In 2015, the National Fallen Firefighters' Foundation identified that First Responders need better resources to cope with duty-related complications.[138] The National Volunteer Fire Council (NVFC) further supported the importance of tailored interventions. In one of their surveys (NVFC, 2008), more than 75% of firefighters indicated greater willingness to utilize a program that was tailored to their needs compared to the National Suicide Hotline.[139]

Unfortunately, most First Responders' departments have limited resources, let alone available interventions tailored to the population. This leaves First Responders feeling unheard and unsupported by the administration. See chapter 10 for ways to find help.

CHAPTER 7 REAL TALK ON SUICIDE

First Responders are twice as likely to experience suicidal thoughts.

Trigger Warning:
Many people with PTSD have thoughts about suicide,
so as uncomfortable as this chapter might be,
we have to discuss it.

A study in the Journal of Safety Research, *An analysis of suicides among First Responders — Findings from the National Violent Death Reporting System, 2015–2017*, examined the factors contributing to higher suicide rates among First Responders:[140]

- Data from the National Violent Death Reporting System (NVDRS) indicates that First Responders made up 1% of all suicides from 2015-2017.
- When broken down by response discipline, these First Responder suicides occurred among law enforcement officers (58%), firefighters (21%), EMS providers (18%) and emergency dispatchers (2%).
- Compared to suicides of non-First Responders, more First Responders used a firearm as the method of injury (69% versus 44%).
- Volunteer Emergency Service Workers have higher rates of depression, suicidal thoughts, and more attempted suicide than paid career firefighters.[141]

- Among First Responder suicides for whom circumstances were known, intimate partner problems, job problems and physical health problems were most frequent.
- Lack of social support is a major factor contributing to feelings of hopelessness and suicide among First Responders.[142]

If you are having suicidal thoughts right now, please contact the National Suicide Prevention Lifeline

988
https://suicidepreventionlifeline.org/

The Lifeline provides 24/7, free, and confidential support for people in distress.

We're going to talk about suicide in a way that acknowledges that many of us with PTSD have either tried to commit suicide or have seriously considered it, ourselves included. It's uncomfortable, but because nothing less than your life is at stake, we won't apologize for what we have to say. Buckle in.

Suicides seldom end the way a person hopes.

It is a violent, messed-up way to die, and everyone who is suicidal already knows that. We *know* this, yet we still think about it.

Suicidal thoughts are an unbelievably normal part of PTSD.

Normal doesn't mean that they are pleasant; it just means

that we can expect this with PTSD - and we need to talk about it because it is the norm and not the exception.

Let's go back to that feelings continuum.

FEELINGS I DON'T WANT TO FEEL				FEELINGS I DO WANT TO FEEL	

←——————————————————————————————————————→

SADNESS, FEAR, GUILT   RAGE, ANGER   SARCASM, "MEH," WHO CARES?   INTEREST, FASCINATION, WONDER   LOVE, JOY

We remember that things on this feelings continuum reduce from both ends in equal measure.

When we avoid those crappy feelings on the left, we become *unable* to feel the good feelings we want on the right. We end up feeling right in the middle: numb.

FEELINGS I DON'T WANT TO FEEL   FEELINGS I DO WANT TO FEEL

←——→
NUMB

Numb is a frightening feeling. We know we should feel something, and we *actually* feel nothing. We may start to ask ourselves questions like, "what is wrong with me?" or "am I a sociopath?" Maybe we start to believe that we will never be "normal" again. We just feel nothing; no joy, no sadness—just numb.

Then we get an idea: I can end all of this by committing suicide. Suddenly we feel *something*—and this is a shock to us because we've felt nothing, absolutely nothing, for a long time. It feels *good*—not because the idea of taking ourselves out of the game isn't gruesome, but because we *feel something* again.

With suicide, we may not have the right answer, but we have something new.

This may give us a little boost in our spirits, maybe some pep in our step.

Our spouse may comment to us that we seem different or our colleagues may say, "it's good to see you smiling," and only we know why. All this external validation feels good, and we start thinking suicide may not be such a bad idea after all.

When therapists talk with a surviving loved one after a suicide, they often hear the same phrases over and over.

"They seemed to be doing so much better lately."

"I saw them smiling and participating in activities."

"We thought the worst was over."

The suicide surprised them because they only saw what was present on the outside.

Sometimes we use thinking about suicide as a coping mechanism, or a strategy that we use in the face of stress to help us manage.

We may draft the suicide letter we will write, or fantasize about who will be at our memorial, or imagine the ways our family and loved ones will be "better off" once we are gone.

Here's the thing, like other coping mechanisms, it *works*. Thinking about suicide can make us feel better and reinforce our belief that suicide is a good idea, even when we know it's not.

We may be telling ourselves, "I'm not going to actually do it, I just think about it." We fantasize about it more and more until we are thinking about suicide all the time. Inevitably, the stress we experience exceeds our capacity to manage it, and we begin to grasp for solutions—any solutions.

"It all happened so fast" is the number one phrase heard after a suicide attempt. We are likely under the influence of alcohol or drugs, and with PTSD, we are **literally** not in our right minds. And it goes down fast.

"Before I knew it, I had the gun in my mouth."

"Before I knew it, I was tying the noose."

"Before I knew it, the bottle of pills was gone."

Fantasy can turn into action at a frightening pace.

We may be telling ourselves that we'll never actually commit suicide, but it's hard to get off a moving train once we feel overwhelmed.

Suicidality doesn't always look like sticking a gun in our mouths. It can be reckless behavior, excessive drinking, or drug use.

This is what we need you to know.

When we're using thoughts of suicide as a coping mechanism, we're closer to the tipping point than we think. It's time to get help.

Suicide: The Forever Decision by Paul G. Quinnett is free to read online and an amazing resource if you are thinking about suicide in any way.[143] Links are in the resource section at the back of this book.

You are not the only person who has thought of suicide or made an attempt in the face of PTSD. This is hard, but as Dr. Quinnett says, suicide is a forever decision.

We've already learned that our PTSD symptoms can fundamentally alter our psyche and our belief systems. Given this, it is highly likely that we are not seeing things for what they are, but we are seeing everything *through the lens of PTSD.*

In other words, it is possible that we are wrong.

Yup, we said it. You could be wrong, friend. Donkey Kong wrong.

We might have convinced ourselves that everyone will be better off if we kill ourselves, and maybe we are wrong, and our death will be a nightmare.

We may think we are beyond help, and maybe we are wrong because we don't know what we don't know.

You might have more grit and determination inside you than you think.

We know you're tired. PTSD is exhausting. But...

Maybe your healing will make you stronger; it might make your family stronger. Maybe—*maybe*—you're reading this for a reason. Maybe we don't need to do this anymore. Change is possible; maybe it's time.

CHAPTER 8 HOW CHANGE HAPPENS

AN INTRODUCTION TO THE "BIG TWO"

TRIGGER WARNING: A lot of you are not going to like what we're about to say (#meanladies). But to recover from PTSD or Moral Injury, we need to start with an honest conversation about our fundamental belief systems. That means honestly asking ourselves the tough questions.

> 1. DO I BELIEVE CHANGE IS POSSIBLE?
>
> 2. DO I WANT TO CHANGE?

These are the Big Two. And as brutal as they are, we must answer them honestly before we start our healing journey.

- If we do not believe change is possible, we're right.
- If we don't want to change, we're wasting our time.

This is a hard truth. The goal of this book is to help you heal, but you have to be willing.

We realize that those questions are not easy to answer. You may be yelling back at us right now,

"You don't understand what I've done, where I've been, how it happened - you don't get it."

You're right; we haven't walked your walk.

What we're asking you to do is have a brutally honest talk with yourself and ask,

"Do I believe that change is possible for me?"

> The reason we ask the Big Two questions is because no therapist, no research – no one and no thing outside of ourselves – can convince us something is true when we fundamentally believe it is not.

Read that text box again.

Q1

"Do I believe that it is possible that I can recover from my PTSD symptoms and reclaim my life?"

We know that's what we want, but this is a different question. We must ask, "do I believe that this is possible *for me*?"

We can expand on this:

- Is it possible that I could get to a point where I'm not thinking about this every single day?
- Do I believe that it's possible for me not to feel suicidal anymore?
- Is it possible that I'm a fundamentally good person and that this PTSD is tricking me into believing I'm not?
- Is it possible that I can learn to understand myself and maybe even forgive myself?
- Do I believe any of this is even possible?

Q2

This one is a bit harder.

"Do I want to change?"

Treatment for PTSD is going to create a lot of change. If we want to reclaim our life, we have to be willing to accept that recovery takes work. Are we willing to do the work that it's going to take? Do we want it badly enough to get out of our comfort zone, to do the difficult thing, if that is what it will take to get better?

> Choosing to go through PTSD treatment involves risk, since successful PTSD treatment requires working with another person—a licensed treatment professional. We have to choose to be our authentic and raw selves with them.

There is no denying that treatment is hard work. Being vulnerable and exposing our truth to another person is frightening. We may feel fear of judgment or reliving the trauma, and that is the fear that has probably kept you in place, suffering with PTSD. Change is frightening, but the rewards are worth the risk. However, only you can decide if you are willing to try.

PTSD treatment affects our lives and our relationships with ourselves and others.

Not everyone is comfortable being wrong, and we may discover in treatment that we have been unfair to ourselves or made assumptions that were not correct. We may need to make amends, or we may need to forgive.

Not everyone who struggles with PTSD believes change is possible. Not everyone wants to change. *And that is okay.* Zero judgement here. We get it.

Maybe you're a spouse or a friend reading this book because you want to help someone you care about, and the idea of your loved one not getting help is not okay with you.

Here's the thing: Yes, it is okay, and we recommend you stand down for your own sanity. This is hard to hear, so we're saying this with love: *You have no control over what someone else believes*. You can't make someone else want to change because that is not how life works. We know this feels unfair because you see how this is affecting your loved one—and you—and we realize this may be tearing you and your family apart.

The fact is that the only person who can change me is me, and the only person who can change you is you.

Are we asking you to give up hope? Absolutely not. We're asking you to recognize that **people get help when** *they* **are ready, not when** *we* **are ready**. And that's okay.

There are many of us reading this who are on the fence about the Big Two questions, and that is okay, too.

It is 100% okay not to feel all-in.

Instead, we'll ask you this: *Is it possible that you are stronger than you think?*

Trauma warps our fundamental belief systems—beliefs about ourselves, others, and the world—and it is possible that our self-doubt is part of the PTSD.

Have you ever done something before that was hard or you felt was impossible at the time? Is it possible that your belief system might be undermining your attempts to make changes? Would you be willing to try to see if you are stronger than you think you are?

Lastly, we need to introduce the elephant in the room.

---

*There are many of us reading this
who don't believe we deserve to recover.*

In counseling hundreds of patients, we have come to see that this belief is not an outlier.

In the Types of Trauma chapter, we talked about Moral Injury. Remember that **Moral Injury is soul damage**. Because of the shame involved, we often can't talk about what happened, so **we can resort to punishing ourselves**.

Sometimes, this self-punishment comes in the form of choosing not to get the treatment we need. We sometimes tell ourselves that we don't deserve to have a life because of what we believe we did or didn't do. We may feel a form of survivor's guilt or tell ourselves that we don't deserve to get better because we are responsible for what happened.

So, we're going to ask you this instead.

Is it possible that you're wrong?

My friend, if you believe that getting treatment is a cop-out or the "easy way" to do things, you need to read on and learn about Evidence-Based Treatment methods.

PTSD treatment is the very definition of taking responsibility. It requires us to stare into the belly of the beast, take full responsibility for our choices, and come face to face with our Truth.

The Truth will set you free. And maybe not in the way you expect.

We understand the existential desire to punish ourselves, but it's likely that you are not seeing your experience from an objective, third-person perspective.

If you believe you don't deserve to get better, that's okay. But we're challenging you to verify that by seeking the truth. Get treatment and then make an informed decision. If you're still hopped up on punishing yourself afterwards, at least you'll be certain why.

But here's the thing, friend: If you've come across one thing in this book that has surprised you so far, it's possible you're wrong about a lot of other stuff, too. Remind us of what you have to lose by getting treatment?

CHAPTER 9 SOLUTIONS

When it comes to PTSD treatment, there are lots of opinions, and you know what they say about opinions, "*Everyone has one, and most of them stink.*" And to add insult to injury, most of these opinions have the word "just" to indicate how easy people think they are.

You just need to exercise more.

You just need to cut out gluten.

You just need to pray.

Before you write us a strongly worded email, we're not saying that getting off your butt, cutting carbs, and getting with a higher power is a bad idea. In fact, we don't think anyone is being malicious when they give their opinion or say what worked for them. We trust Evidence-Based Treatments.

Here's the thing, we talked about these kinds of Toxic Positivity statements in an earlier chapter (See Types of Trauma in Chapter 3). They come from a place of uncertainty. The person giving that advice doesn't know how to help you, but they want to feel like they are helpful.

If you want real help, it is going to come from a licensed therapist in the form of an Evidence-Based Treatment (EBTs).

EBTs are based on peer-reviewed scientific evidence. This means that researchers have conducted rigorous studies using scientific methods, documented their research in peer-reviewed publications, and then other researchers have conducted additional studies to see if the treatment is, in fact, successful. Unlike anecdotes, a ton of time and research goes into verifying that EBTs work. There is verifiable proof of this. EBTs work **most of the time for most people**, and they do so in about 12 sessions.

Three of the most commonly employed Evidence-Based Treatments for PTSD are:

- **Prolonged Exposure Therapy (PE)**
- **Cognitive Processing Therapy (CPT)**
- **Eye-Movement Desensitization and Reprocessing (EMDR)**

We encourage you to ask for these EBTs by name and be insistent. Other clinical practice guidelines for the treatment of PTSD, recommends the three above named specific trauma-focused psychotherapies, as the most effective treatments for PTSD.

In some cases, the above-mentioned individual trauma-focused psychotherapies may not be available in all settings, and not all patients choose to engage in these treatments. There are several other trauma-specific manualized cognitive behavioral therapy protocols that are suggested to reduce symptoms of PTSD such as, Cognitive Therapy, Written Exposure Therapy (WET), and Present Centered Therapy (PCT).

That said, there is no sense in working with a therapist who is not specifically trained in how to treat PTSD. It's a waste of time and leads to even more frustration.

Researchers also know that there is a certain percentage of folks whose PTSD won't respond to these three EBTs. That doesn't mean that you're beyond hope, it just means we need to find another avenue of approach. There is a lot of money in PTSD research, and a lot of good clinical trials and solutions to try.

As of this writing, here are some of the treatments for treatment-resistant PTSD being used:

- The stellate ganglion block (sometimes called the "God Shot")
- Ketamine
- Marijuana
- Hallucinogens like MDMA
- Couples therapy

There are various treatments that help with PTSD and co-occurring disorders like depression, alcohol use, anger, anxiety, and TBIs.

These include Accelerated Resolution Therapy (ART), Adaptive Disclosure (AD), Acceptance and Commitment Therapy (ACT), Brief Eclectic Psychotherapy (BEP), Dialectical Behavior Therapy (DBT), Emotional Freedom Techniques (EFT), Impact on Killing (IoK), Interpersonal Psychotherapy (IPT), Narrative Exposure Therapy (NET), Prolonged Exposure in Primary Care (PE-PC), psychodynamic therapy, psychoeducation, Reconsolidation of Traumatic Memories (RTM), Seeking Safety (SS), Stress Inoculation Training (SIT), Skills Training in Affective and Interpersonal Regulation (STAIR), Skills Training in Affective and Interpersonal Regulation in Primary Care (STAIR-PC), supportive counseling, Thought Field Therapy (TFT), Trauma-Informed Guilt Reduction (TRiGR), or Trauma Management Therapy.

This list is by no means exhaustive; researchers are learning more every day.

The point is, there are options available to help you with

PTSD!

For now, we're going to assume that you have not tried any EBTs yet. Since most EBTs work for most people, we're going to explain each of the three main treatments to help you make an informed decision. Therapy is not easy, but it's not forever, either.

PROLONGED EXPOSURE THERAPY (PE)

PE Therapy typically takes 10-15 sessions with a therapist; each session is 90 minutes. PE therapy goes right for the jugular of criterion C of PTSD: Avoidance.

Rather than avoid our trauma, we intentionally invite the most traumatic event into the session using a technique called "imaginal exposure." After learning breathing techniques to manage anxiety, we imagine and describe the traumatic event in detail with guidance from a therapist. After the imaginal exposure, we process the experience with our therapist. We audio record the session while describing the event so that we can listen to the recording between sessions. This helps us to further process our emotions and practice breathing techniques. Think of the imaginal exposure like this; it's like watching a horror movie.

When we first watch a horror movie, it scares the crap out of us because that's what horror movies do. What if we watch the horror movie back-to-back three times?

It's still going to be scary, but, after the third time, we know what is coming and when, so it's not as bad as the first time.

What if we watch that horror movie ten times? Twenty times? A hundred times? Eventually, watching that movie doesn't affect us as much because we've seen it so many times and we know what's coming. This is called habituation; a decrease in response to a stimulus after repeated presentations.

In PE therapy, we'll be watching our horror movie literally hundreds of times—in session with our therapist and in between sessions by listening to our recordings.

The second part of PE therapy is called *in vivo exposure*, a fancy term for "in real life." With our therapist, we make a list of stimuli and situations connected to our trauma, such as specific places or people, and create a plan to intentionally expose ourselves to these stimuli in a way that is gradual and safe.

We realize that the thought of retelling our experience out loud can be anxiety-provoking. It's tough, especially at the start, but PE therapy is undeniably effective. It also can be adapted into treatment for Moral Injury, which we'll talk about later in this chapter.

PE therapy isn't for everyone, and that's okay because we're discussing three available EBTs, not just one. Here's the second.

COGNITIVE PROCESSING THERAPY (CPT)

CPT typically takes 12 sessions with a therapist; each session is 60 minutes. CPT can be done individually or in group sessions, and it uses a workbook for written assignments. "Cognitive" means that we pay attention to our thoughts and *think about what we are thinking about.*

CPT recognizes that trauma warps our fundamental belief systems—beliefs about ourselves, others, and the world—and that those warped beliefs affect our walking, talking, everyday lives.

In CPT, we learn about the relationship between thoughts and emotions and then learn to identify the automatic thoughts that maintain our PTSD symptoms.

We write an "impact statement" that details our understanding of why the traumatic event occurred and what impact it has had on our belief systems.

Next, we'll use workbook exercises to identify and address unhelpful thinking patterns related to safety, trust, power and control, esteem, and intimacy.

Our therapist will ask questions and work with us to recognize unhelpful thinking patterns, reframe our thoughts, reduce our symptoms, and come to a better understanding about ourselves and our relationships.

CPT forces us to get out of "auto-pilot" and start challenging our thought patterns.

Often these are thoughts we have held onto for a long time.

EYE-MOVEMENT DESENSITIZATION AND REPROCESSING (EMDR)

This description is from the good folks at the EMDR Institute, found online at www.emdr.com, and we encourage you to find a therapist who practices EMDR to give you a better description than the one provided.

EMDR is an eight-phase treatment that focuses attention on three distinct time periods: the past, present, and future. Sessions often last between 60-90 minutes.

The eight phases include:

History-taking: In this phase, the therapist obtains a detailed history of the client's past memories and current struggles. During this phase, the therapist will try and identify targets for the EMDR processing. These can be distressing memories or incidents.

Client preparation: This is where the client learns techniques for active healing trauma processing. The therapist will go over strategies, suggest relaxation techniques, and other coping strategies that can help their client deal with emotional distress and maintain improvements as the sessions progress.

Assessment: In this phase, the client is asked to picture an image closely related to the target memory and to elicit the negative response and beliefs associated with the memory. The client is also asked to identify a positive belief that they would like to believe instead.

Desensitization: The therapist asks their client to focus on a specific memory, belief, or emotional trigger while simultaneously engaging in bilateral stimulation (BLS).

BLS consists of alternating right and left stimulation, whether it's tapping of the toes or tapping on the shoulders. It can also include audio or visual stimulation with the use of light. This stimulation may include eye movements, taps, or tones.

It is believed that BLS used in EMDR activates both hemispheres of the brain, which is believed to have a soothing effect, and dim the intensity of the memory while allowing the client space to process it without an overwhelming psychological response. This continues until that memory is no longer triggering for the client.

Installation: With the help of the therapist, this is where the client starts to replace negative thoughts with positive ones. Continuing to review the triggering memory with BLS, the client is asked to assess the emotional response and rate it against the positive belief (brought up during the assessment phase) they would prefer to associate it with.

Body scan: Here, the client is assessed for changes in body sensations when thinking of the negative incident and positive thought. Any remaining tension in the body is targeted by the therapist for additional processing.

Closure: Clients will be asked to write down any thoughts or emotions that arise during the coming week, and will be reminded of the self-soothing techniques they learned during the session in order to process any negative thoughts that may surface.

Reevaluation: This phase is to review and/or assess for other targets that cause distressing emotion within the chosen memory.

PERSISTENCE

Don't stress out about which EBT to choose. Most cognitive-behavior therapies for PTSD work by exposing clients repeatedly to anxiety-provoking stimuli, either in their imagination (imaginal exposure) or in real life (in vivo exposure). When exposure to either type is sufficiently prolonged, clients' anxiety dissipates.

If we try one and it doesn't work, we have two more to fall back on. If we try all three and they don't work, we may be dealing with complex PTSD, treatment-resistant PTSD, or have co-occurring disorders to work through. Do not lose hope. This simply means we have a little more work to do with our treatment professional to come up with a more targeted course of action.

Numerous factors influence treatment outcomes, and no single treatment, or Evidence-Based Treatment has demonstrated 100% effectiveness for every single person with PTSD. That doesn't mean recovery is hopeless. It's just going to take a little more work.

Let's go back to those earlier questions.

> 1. DO I BELIEVE CHANGE IS POSSIBLE?
>
> 2. DO I WANT TO CHANGE?

The goal of this book is to help you heal, but you have to be willing even when it is tough.

We know you don't want to hear that and believe us when we say we empathize.

That also means we know sugarcoating or trying to downplay the possibility that PTSD treatments might take a little longer than expected is not doing you any favors.

If "knowing is half the battle," we want you to win the war.

And that means arming you with all the facts so you can get the help you need.

So, what could be delaying our recovery? The type and duration of trauma seems to play a part in the success of recovery.

It is also common for PTSD to be accompanied by comorbid psychiatric conditions, including depression, Substance Use Disorder, and somatic symptoms making diagnosing the correct type of PTSD and any associating conditions key in unlocking the correct combination of treatments.

We realize that the idea of going through treatment for PTSD and still having to do more work is frustrating. Having more work to do doesn't mean we failed; it just means we have more work to do and that's okay.

Be easier on yourself; Rome wasn't built in a day.

CHAPTER 10 HOW TO FIND HELP

Now that we understand PTSD and the Evidence-Based Treatments that help, we need to find someone to help us create and execute a plan of action.

FINDING A THERAPIST

We understand that many of us do not relish the idea of going to therapy. The terms "therapy" and "counseling" are largely interchangeable. We might have the idea that we'll have to lie down on a couch and talk about our mommy issues, or maybe we think therapy is only for crazy people.

Obviously, we'd prefer to do it on our own rather than find a therapist. We get that, but there is tremendous value in **NOT** doing this alone and instead working with a licensed mental health professional. It is valuable to get feedback from someone who can provide an objective, third-person perspective, who is 100% on our side, and sincerely wants what is best for us.

Moreover, our therapist is not our friend. This is a good thing to understand because a therapist can tell us what we *need* to hear instead of what we *want* to hear.

Our therapist will not always agree with us and will often challenge our understanding, point out negative self-talk, and ask us tough questions.

The word "therapist" is a generic term for someone who conducts therapy with clients. Many mental health professionals fall into this category. If possible, we recommend finding a licensed therapist with specialized training in treating PTSD; a specialist, and not a generalist.

When someone has cancer, they don't go to their family doctor for treatment. They go to an oncologist, someone who specializes in cancer. When our life is on the line, we want the best possible treatment. The same is true for mental health. Therapists tend to specialize in specific treatment methods or specific client populations.

For example, Virginia focuses on combat-related PTSD and Moral Injury. While she can do other things, it's not what she's best at. She has amazing colleagues who specialize in eating disorders, adolescent issues, depression, anxiety, and all manner of mental health issues. If you come into her office with an experience that is better addressed with one of her colleagues, she will refer you to them.

Finding a therapist who specializes in PTSD and has training in an Evidence-Based Treatment for PTSD is smart, but it isn't always easy. To find a PTSD specialist, we can get help from our health insurer's website or use our company's Employee Assistance Program (EAP).

You can also use the following resources to get you started on your search.

NVFC Directory of Behavioral Health Professionals
https://www.nvfc.org/provider-directory/
The providers listed in this directory are behavioral health professionals vetted by the Firefighter Behavioral Health Alliance (FBHA). This directory is updated on a monthly basis.

Behavioral Health Treatment Services Locator (USA)
https://findtreatment.gov/
This is a government-run online database of mental health and substance abuse treatment facilities, both inpatient and outpatient. The database is searchable by location and type of treatment needed.

EMDR Licensed Clinician Search
https://www.emdr.com/
Tool from the EMDR Institute that allows you to search for clinicians that have been trained and licensed to use EMDR. EMDR is a type of therapy that has been shown to be beneficial in treating traumatic stress and PTSD.

AMR's EAP – 1-888-327-0024 or 1-888-327-1060
Employee Assistance Program for American Medical Response employees in the US and the phone number to the 24/7 crisis/counseling line. The phone number should be used if you need help ASAP.

Once we find a therapist, we can call and request a phone consultation with them. Keep in mind that we may call and leave messages with several providers, but may only hear back from a few. (Therapists can be crappy this way.)

During the phone consult:

1. Briefly explain why we are seeking therapy.

2. Ask what experience they have in treating clients like us.

3. Ask if they are trained in Evidence-Based Treatments for PTSD/Moral Injury.

This may sound like:

"I'm a First Responder and I'm struggling to cope with the work stress. What kind of treatment do you use for PTSD?"

If the therapist does not have training in an Evidence-Based Treatment for PTSD, ask them if they can recommend someone who does.

Next, we'll make our first appointment. It's okay to feel nervous. In this first session, we are getting to know the therapist and trying to determine if it is a relationship that will last.

It also might not be. Not all therapists are compatible with all clients, and that's okay. The relationship between a client and their therapist is important. We need to feel a sense of trust with our therapist because we have to choose to be authentic in order to improve.

Some therapists are unprofessional or simply not good at their jobs. We're not trying to be ugly. It is what it is. If you don't click with your therapist, it's not necessarily you. Keep looking. There is excellent advice online about how to choose the best therapist.[144]

Having a therapist we can trust is an important cornerstone for our social support network and is vital to our recovery.

TALK TO YOUR THERAPIST ABOUT CONFIDENTIALITY

The Health Insurance Portability and Accountability Act (HIPAA) contains a privacy rule that creates national standards to protect individuals' medical records and personal health information, including information about psychotherapy and mental health.

HIPAA privacy is a limited level of protection only.

Confidentiality is one reason therapy works. Therapists understand that for people to feel comfortable talking about private and revealing information, they need a safe place to talk about anything, without fear of that information leaving the room. And they take patient confidentiality seriously. However, the limits of confidentiality in counseling stop whenever a client expresses the intent to harm themselves or others. In those situations, the therapist is legally obligated to break confidentiality.

According to the privacy and confidentiality section of the APA's ethical code of conduct for therapists, there are four general situations which are exempt from confidentiality:[145]

- The client is an imminent and violent threat towards themselves or others.
- There is a billing situation which requires a condoned disclosure.
- Sharing information is necessary to facilitate client care across multiple providers.
- Sharing information is necessary to treat the client.

At your first visit, the therapist should give you information that explains their privacy policies and how your personal information will be handled.

This information will explain that, in some cases, there are exceptions to the privacy rule:

- The therapist may disclose private information without consent in order to protect the patient or the public from serious harm—if, for example, a client discusses plans to attempt suicide or harm another person.
- The therapist is required to report abuse or neglect of children, the elderly, or people with disabilities.
- The therapist may release information if they receive a court order.

A good therapist should be happy to go over any confidentiality concerns with you before starting therapy. Ask any questions at that time, to put your mind at ease. Some questions we suggest asking are:

- Who will have access to your clinical notes?
- What do you report to my health insurance?
- What is the level of detail you will document in my medical records?

We encourage asking for a copy of your medical records. You should read them, too.

Remember, your therapist should be transparent.
If they aren't, it's time to find a new therapist.

PEER SUPPORT GROUPS

Peer support is when people with similar experiences, whether it's their own mental health challenges or those of a loved one, come together to provide each other with support and understanding.

Many First Responder organizations are starting to use peer support as a way to help their employees deal with the stress and trauma they experience on the job.

This can include things like Critical Incident Stress Management (CISM), where support is provided after a particularly difficult event.

Workplace-based peer support is a specific type of peer support where employees who have gone through their own mental health struggles receive special training to support their coworkers.

The main goal of peer support is to offer hope and promote recovery for those dealing with mental health challenges. These programs are often led by people who may not be licensed therapists, but who have been trained to listen and facilitate group healing sessions.

Peer support can have many benefits, including:

- Humanizing mental health issues.
- Reducing feelings of isolation.
- Helping people gain control over their symptoms.
- Promoting hope and resilience.
- Increasing understanding of mental health within an organization.

It also allows peers to connect and work towards common goals, improving the overall quality of life for everyone involved. And let's not forget the rewarding experience for those providing the support. Listening and helping others can be healing in itself.

Here are a few to get you started:

American Academy of Experts in Traumatic Stress
https://www.aaets.org/frontline-groups
Their goal is to coordinate efforts to increase the support available to healthcare workers and emergency responders.

How2LoveOurCops
https://www.how2loveourcops.org/
A 501(c)(3) organization that is dedicated to the relational, emotional and spiritual wellness of law enforcement families.

NAMI Peer Support Resources
https://www.nami.org/Your-Journey/Frontline-Professionals/Public-Safety-Professionals/Peer-Support-Resources

The Wounded Blue
https://thewoundedblue.org/services/
The Wounded Blue is working to de-stigmatize mental health within the law enforcement community through its Peer Advocate Support Program and community outreach.

The Disaster Responder Assets Network (DRAN)
https://disasterassets.org/
The Disaster Responder Assets Network (DRAN) is a volunteer non-profit (501c3) organization comprised of men and women that have dedicated their lives to the service of others.

First Responder Support Network
https://www.frsn.org/
A program dedicated to supporting the mental health and well-being of all First Responders and their families.

Next Rung
https://www.nextrung.org/
Offers free peer support via talk, text, social media messaging, email, Skype, or FaceTime. If you are in immediate need of help, please text "SUPPORT" to 1-833-NXT-RUNG (698-7864).

Hope for Emergency Responders Organization (HERO)
https://herofirst.org/
Peer Support For First Responders.

Survivor's Network for Air & Surface Medical Transport
https://www.survivorsnetwork-airmedical.org/
This network provides support, education, and resources to air & surface medical organizations, personnel, and their families.

SAMHSA
https://www.samhsa.gov/
Lots of resources here.
Survivors of Loved Ones' Suicides (SOLOS)
https://www.solossa.org/
is an especially powerful peer-led support group.

A WORD ON SUPPORT GROUPS AND GROUP THERAPY

Support groups are often led by paraprofessionals rather than licensed therapists.

We're **huge** proponents of group therapy.

Before sharing your Truth, we encourage you to (1) ensure that your group is run by an experienced group leader, preferably a certified group psychotherapist, and (2) to discuss confidentiality with your therapist and with your therapy group.[146]

We cannot guarantee confidentiality in groups because other group members are not mental health professionals required to follow the rules of ethics in order to keep a state license. Unfortunately, this makes sharing our Truth in groups a risk we must seriously consider.

GROUP THERAPY

Therapy groups, unlike support groups, are led by licensed mental health professionals, and they can be effective methods of support. There are marked differences between group therapy and support groups. Therapy groups tend to be small, with around eight group members and one or two group leaders.

The leaders screen group members prior to members joining the group, and leaders are licensed mental health providers with group training.

Group therapy is not free. It is sometimes covered by health insurance or members pay out of pocket.

Groups can be online or in person. Group is hard work, and it's worth it.

HOW TO GET MENTAL HEALTH HELP WITH LITTLE TO NO INSURANCE

- A distressingly large number of people with mental health issues have little to no insurance.[147]
- 11.1% of Americans with a mental illness are uninsured.
- 8.1% of children have private insurance that does not cover mental health services.
- In 2019, 24.7% of adults with a mental illness reported an unmet need for treatment.
- Over half of adults with a mental illness do not receive treatment, totaling over 27 million untreated adults in the US.

The sad truth is, many Americans struggle to pay for expensive mental health treatment with little or no insurance coverage, and First Responders are included in this group. Many First Responders resort to paying out of pocket for a specialist when company provided resources are inadequate or simply not available.

There is help out there.

Please use the following list to get you started:

988 Suicide and Crisis Line
The Lifeline provides 24/7, free and confidential support for people in distress, prevention and crisis resources for you or your loved ones, and best practices for professionals in the United States.

Safe Call Now – 1-206-459-3020
A 24/7 help line staffed by First Responders for First Responders and their family members. They can assist with treatment options for responders who are suffering from mental health, substance abuse and other personal issues.

Fire/EMS Helpline – 1-888-731-3473
Also known as Share The Load. A program run by the National Volunteer Fire Council. They have a help line, text-based help service, and have also collected a list of many good resources for people looking for help and support.

Crisis Text Line
A service that allows people in crisis to speak with a trained crisis counselor by texting "Start" or "Help" to 741-741.

Copline (Law Enforcement Only) – 1-800-267-5463
A confidential helpline for members of US law enforcement. Their website also has additional information on help and resources.

Frontline Helpline – 1-866-676-7500
Run by Frontline Responder Services. Offer 24/7 coverage with First Responder call-takers.

Kristin Brooks Hopeline – 1-800-442-4673
Another national (USA) hotline for people suffering from mental health issues.

Suicide.org
http://suicide.org/
List of local helplines for all 50 states. This list includes thousands of local call numbers for every state in the US. Calling a local number can help put you in contact with nearby resources like counselors or psychiatrists faster than calling a national line.

Gary Sinise Foundation
https://www.garysinisefoundation.org/first-responders-outreach/
Offers grants up to $50,000 for First Responder agencies and First Responders who need assistance paying for equipment, training, medical expenses related to line-of-duty-injuries, and home modifications due to permanent disabilities.

PsyberGuide
https://psyberguide.org/

Website that rates a large number of mental health apps. Also contains lists of apps designed for specific conditions and apps that follow a specific treatment modality.

7 Cups
https://www.7cups.com/
Website/App – Utilizes both trained listeners and licensed therapists and counselors to provide services. Trained listeners are laypeople trained in active listening who provide free confidential support.

Users can also establish a relationship with a licensed professional for a fee. Not First Responder specific, but they allow you to pick your listener and therapist so you can find someone who you're likely to be able to connect with.

IntelliCare
https://intellicare.cbits.northwestern.edu/
App (Android only) – IntelliCare is a suite of apps that work together to target common causes of depression and anxiety like sleep problems, social isolation, lack of activity, and obsessive thinking.

These apps are part of a nationwide research study funded by the National Institutes of Health.

PTSD Coach
https://www.ptsd.va.gov/public/materials/apps/ptsdcoach.asp
Website/App – Designed by the National Center for PTSD (a division of the VA). PTSD Coach provides information about diagnosing and treating PTSD, the ability to track symptoms, information on handling stress, and direct links to support and help. Canadian version in French available for iPhone.

Lighthouse Health & Wellness
https://www.lighthousehw.org/
Lighthouse Health & Wellness is an in-hand, on-demand, 100% confidential health and wellness platform available at no cost to our nation's public safety agencies.

CHAPTER 11 SOCIAL SUPPORT

THE POWER OF SOCIAL SUPPORT

Having a strong support system can make a world of difference in our lives. Whether we are facing challenges or simply need someone to confide in, having people who support and care for us can greatly impact our overall well-being. Recent studies have shown that social support not only helps us cope with tough times but also plays a vital role in promoting mental wellness and protecting against distress. This is especially significant for individuals who have experienced trauma. The power of social support should never be underestimated, especially in times of hardship. It has proven to be a major factor in aiding individuals in recovering from difficult events.[148]

There are three main types of social support:[149]

- Emotional support involves providing trust, empathy, love, and care for the person seeking help. This type of support can help individuals feel less alone and improve their overall sense of well-being.
- Instrumental support, on the other hand, involves providing practical assistance. This can include financial aid or help with daily tasks, which may be essential for those with immediate needs. Studies have shown that instrumental support is associated with a lower risk of suicide death.

- Informational support involves offering advice and guidance. This can help individuals make informed decisions and access appropriate resources for coping with their trauma.

Studies have shown that those with larger social networks and those who feel supported experience less reactivity to stressors and have better mental health overall. This supports the "stress-buffering hypothesis," which proposes that having strong social support can help reduce negative thoughts and beliefs following a traumatic experience. Essentially, social support acts as a shield against stress, making traumatic experiences seem less impactful while providing valuable coping resources.[150]

Remember, whether it comes from a romantic partner, family member, close friend, or support group, having reliable and effective social support has been identified as one of the most significant contributors to overall well-being.

BUILDING SOCIAL SUPPORT

"Social Support." This is what mental health professionals call friends and researchers have shown over and again the importance of social support in treating PTSD. Our therapist is part of our support team, and we have to build on this foundation. Making friends is difficult, especially if we have PTSD. So, let's talk about it.

Back in the day, making friends was easy. As a kid, we made friends in school or in our neighborhood. And on the job, we have our "work friends." Mostly because we're forced to see the same people every day. And for the most part, our work friends become close friends.

When it comes to PTSD, we all tend to isolate ourselves in the face of PTSD, saying things like, "I don't want to bother them with this. They have their own crap they're going through. My friends are all just so busy. I don't want them to think I'm a drama bomb."

Real talk, if you would drop everything for a friend that is going through what you are going through, then give them the same respect to come and help you.

Making new friends gets harder as we get older. We realize that it's weird to approach a stranger out of the blue and say, "Want to hang out?"

I got anxiety just typing that sentence.

Some people are natural extroverts (and yay for you), but for the rest of us, we worry about making new friends, especially if our PTSD has poisoned our other relationships. It's normal to worry.

"What if new people learn about my PTSD and freak out?"

"What if I have a melt-down, or if I hurt someone by accident?"

"Maybe I'm better off protecting the world by keeping to myself because people have their own problems and they don't need mine."

We hear you, friend, and want to put this into perspective. Trying to make friends is a big risk.

We can be rejected, others can judge us and be crappy, and we might be terrible at making new friends.

But, we also know that social support is a major determining factor in our recovery from PTSD. In other words, to get better, this is a risk we *need* to take.

Because this is important, we want to take you back to the Big Two questions.

(Q1) Do we believe it's possible? Do we believe it's possible that we could get out of our comfort zone, break out of that Criterion C of Avoidance, and connect with another person, either in-person or virtually?

Is it possible that there is another person in this world who is not crappy?

Is it possible that we can use this powerful—and proven—tool of social support to fight our PTSD symptoms?

Is it possible that we deserve to be loved and cared for by others?

That last one is hard with all that Criterion D: Negative self-talk rattling around in our brains.

Remember, we're just asking *if it's possible.*

Trust is hard, especially if, in our past, we've tried to connect with someone for support and they screwed us over.

Moving on to (Q2), "Do we want to change?"

But rephrasing it differently. The second question can't be, "Do we want to make friends?" Because we already know the answer. *"No!"*

With PTSD, we *want* to avoid other people. This is good old criterion C: Avoidance.

It's like asking, "Do we want to go to therapy?"

"Big NO!"

So, we need to look at the bigger picture of Q2.

Do we want to do the work it will take to recover from PTSD?

Do we want to lessen our symptoms?

Do we want the people we love to know that we love them?

Do we want to build, or possibly rebuild, relationships?

It's okay to be on the struggle bus about this. Going to therapy and making connections is difficult when we have PTSD, but we have to do it if we are serious about getting our lives back.

Let's talk about how to do this.

DIFFERENT KINDS OF FRIENDS

When we think about friends, we tend to put them in two categories: (1) lifelong, know everything about me, ride-or-die friends, and (2) acquaintances. Maybe we work with them, and that's about it.

For the purpose of making new friends, we want to introduce a new relationship into our lexicon.

The In-Between Friend.
Not a life-long, ride-or-die friend, and not that weird guy in the office, but something in-between.

As adults, one way we build social support is by making in-between friends.

In-between friends start out just like us; they are other people who are also trying to find social support. Not every in-between friend will turn into a lifelong ride-or-die friend. In fact, most won't. But some of them will. It's the law of averages. The more in-between friends we make, the better the chances of that friendship developing into a ride-or-die friendship.

We recommend that we make this our course of action for building social support. There is little pressure when making in-between friends because the way we find them is to *intentionally go* to places where other people are trying to make in-between friends. We go intending to connect with other like-minded people. And, over time, there is a likelihood that we will *regularly connect* with them.

First things first: What are places or events where people intentionally come together because they want connection?

These are smaller groups (maybe 5-10 people) in which it is likely we will be individually noticed and talk to someone else because it would be hard not to. Everyone attends the group because we all have the intention of connecting with others who have shared values and interests.

These are places where *individuals* come together, not couples or groups of friends.

Sure, we will be the new person the first time we visit the group, but everyone else will have had that same experience at one time. It is largely their role to engage you because they remember how awkward it was for them the first time.

Also, we are looking for groups where there is a **planned activity**. This eliminates anxiety-provoking small talk and the desire to drink or use to feel more comfortable. We don't have to talk about ourselves because we can talk about the activity, and focusing on that activity keeps us from thinking about our PTSD. There is little pressure.

Here is a non-exhaustive list of ideas for finding small groups:

MEETUP

Meetup is a service used to organize online groups that host in-person events for people with similar interests and has over 35 million members.

Their motto is, "We are what we do," and the groups are activity-based. We can look up groups in our area from the comfort and anonymity of the internet at www.meetup.com.

Book clubs, hiking groups, music nerds, museum visiting groups, and pretty much anything you can think of. Their purpose is to meet people in person and spend time together sharing an activity.

Fun fact: Virginia found a photography meetup group in Paris a few years back. They even have an app for smart phones.

CIVIC GROUPS

These are organizations that promote civic or social interests and are often supported by a group of members. Examples are Rotary International, Shriners, Toastmasters, and Veterans groups like the American Legion or the VFW.

Civic groups often support service projects and have guest speakers and networking events.

PROFESSIONAL ORGANIZATIONS

These groups often have networking events rather than specific activities. If shoptalk comes easier to us than feelings-talk, this is a good place to start. Google a specific profession or interest with the phrase "professional organization." Examples are the Veterans Business Network, the National Association for Women Business Owners, the Gay and Lesbian Medical Association, and the National Society of Black Engineers. Local chapters abound.

PLACES OF WORSHIP

Churches, synagogues, ashrams, mosques, and even meet up groups for atheists and agnostics are all places where people come together with a shared belief system. Many places of worship have smaller groups of 5-10 people where we can meet others for a shared activity. Examples are religious study groups, reading groups, home cell groups, choirs and creative arts groups, and community volunteer groups.

Many places of worship have websites and calendars advertising their group events. If not, we recommend looking up the phone number and asking to speak with someone.

Try this script.

"Hi, I'm looking to learn more about your organization and was wondering if you have a small group or event during the week that I could check out to meet some new people."

VOLUNTEERING

Not good with people at all? Us, too. Virginia walks dogs at the local animal shelter and meets other folks who prefer canines to humans.

Volunteering is a great way to meet people who care about the same things we do. We can volunteer to build houses for Vets or organize for social justice.

AA, NA, AL ANON, ETC.

12-step programs are powerful in terms of providing social support and accountability, and there are anonymous groups for many addictions. In addition to the three most widely known programs, Codependents Anonymous (CoDA) is a powerful change agent, as are groups for Gambling and Survivors of Incest.

Not everyone is a fan of the program, and we get it—there are plenty of lousy groups and crappy sponsors. There are also dynamic, inspiring groups, and amazing sponsors. We can group hop until we find a group that suits us.

ONLINE GROUPS

There is an impressive amount of social support available online in chat forums and social media groups. To find one, try using a search term like "online support group PTSD."

Once we find a group we might like, we have to commit to go. The next step is to attend regularly.

Our goal is to make in-between friends, with a long-term goal of building a tribe of supporters.

Tribes come with accountability. When we miss a book club meeting, our in-between friend will call to see if we're sick. When we miss a program meeting, our sponsor will call to see if we've relapsed.

We know that with PTSD we just want to be left alone, but others checking up on us is a good thing. It is the opposite of avoidance because we are intentionally inviting others into our world, even if it's only once a week. Building a social support network is a leap of faith. It's also evidence-based in terms of helping us recover. When we believe change is possible and we want to change, we choose to act. So, (1) pick an activity, and (2) show up. Everyone in the group has been the new person before, they get it.

CHAPTER 12 TALKING ABOUT OUR PTSD

Not everyone has earned the right to know our story, but there are probably some people in our lives who have. In this chapter, we're going to map out exactly how to talk to the people in our lives who matter. We will learn what to say and how to say it.

WE CONTROL THE NARRATIVE OR THE NARRATIVE CONTROLS US

SCIENCE

Let's start by showing you how powerful and transformative our narrative can be.

In 1964, Harvard professor Robert Rosenthal conducted an experiment at an elementary school near San Francisco.[151] He gave all the students a standardized IQ test, but put a new cover sheet on it, calling it the "Harvard Test of Inflected Acquisition." Just to be clear, *this was a lie*. It was a standard IQ test, but Rosenthal gave everyone the impression it was something new and fancy.

Rosenthal told the teachers that this fancy-dancy Harvard test had the ability to predict which kids were about to experience a dramatic growth in their IQ—special kids that were about to get dramatically smarter. Sounds impressive, right? Exactly. *Again, not true.*

After the kids took the test, Rosenthal chose kids completely at random and told their teachers that the test results predicted which kids were on the verge of an intense intellectual bloom. He told the teachers, but not the students. Rosenthal's team followed the children over the next two years, and at the end of the study, all students were tested again with the same IQ-test used at the beginning of the study. Something miraculous happened. The children Rosenthal labeled as "intellectual bloomers" did show statistically significant gains on the test.

Just one problem: These kids were picked at random. How did they experience such a shift in IQ? Rosenthal observed the students in the classroom and discovered that the teacher's expectations significantly affected the students. The teachers' moment-to-moment interactions with the children they expected to bloom differed from the students they considered "normal." Teachers gave the students they expected to succeed _more_ - more individual attention, more time to answer questions, and more affirmation and approval. "It's not magic, it's not mental telepathy," Rosenthal said. "It's very likely these thousands of different ways of treating people, in small ways, every day."

It was not the children's aptitude that gave them a statistically significant improvement in IQ. It was **their narrative**—the story their teachers **believed** about them.

LITERATURE

Let's think about stories that inspire us. Whether fiction or non-fiction, studies of literature tell us that inspirational stories have a similar pattern.

We can go all intel and graph it.

We'll call our X axis "time" and our Y axis "level of happiness/success."

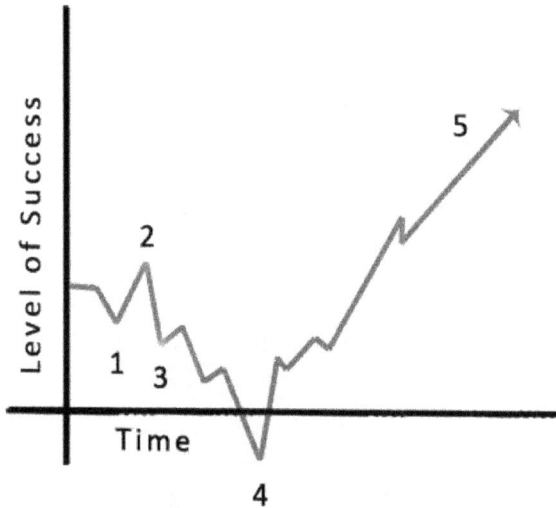

Follow the numbers on the graph and let us show you the basic structure of an inspirational story.

1. So, there I was, doing my own thing, and I failed.

2. I did what I could to get better, and it looked like it was working.

3. But I failed again. I tried and tried, and things kept getting worse.

4. Finally, I hit "rock bottom" and everything went to hell. But at rock bottom, something miraculous happened. I had an epiphany! I learned something I didn't know before, met someone I hadn't met before, did something I'd never done before, and I learned and improved!

5. Because life is life, there were ups and downs, but in general, my life kept going up and I lived happily ever after.

Generally, this is the pattern of stories of people that inspire us. Novelists know this. Every *Chicken Soup for the Soul* book thrives on this, and we feel inspired when we learn about people whose lives fit into this pattern, too. Everyone loves an underdog, everyone loves to see a comeback.

Narratives inspire us and capture our imagination. In controlling our own narrative, we can tap into this power and use it to help gather support from our peers and loved ones as we recover from PTSD.

PSYCHOLOGY

Let's look at an entire school of therapy that focuses on narrative, called Logotherapy.[152] It was developed by Viktor Frankl, a neurologist, psychiatrist, and Auschwitz survivor. Frankl knew that personal experiences are transformed into personal stories that are given meaning and help shape a person's identity.

Frankl understood that there are a lot of things in our lives that we don't get to choose. We don't choose our family or where we grow up; children have precious little autonomy. As adults, we don't always get a choice, either; Frankl certainly did not choose to be imprisoned in a concentration camp.

But Frankl knew that man is "capable of resisting and braving even the worst conditions," and, in doing such, we can detach from situations and from ourselves. Narrative Therapy, credited to Michael White and David Epston, also seeks to externalize situations from ourselves.[153] The idea is that we can choose an attitude about ourselves and our trauma because we survived it.

When we survive it, we get to define it.

We say again: When we survive it, we get to define it. We get to define our trauma, its meaning, and how it shapes us. Nobody else has the right to define our experience because this is not a team sport.

When we tell our story, it is taking an action toward change. Through this third-person point-of-view, we can be more objective. We can have compassion for ourselves while boldly asking for that same compassion and support from others.

OPENING UP ABOUT OUR PTSD TO RECOVER OUR RELATIONSHIPS

This part is uncomfortable, and it should be. Our loved ones matter, and our PTSD has probably messed up some of our most important relationships. We are going to take ownership of our narrative and learn how to openly discuss our issues in a way that creates opportunities to recover our relationships.

Virginia has taught this subject hundreds of times over the last few years and created an "elevator speech." It's based on good science and she's seen it work time and again. We may think that our relationships are too far gone and that we are the one person who cannot make this chapter work, but we have nothing to lose and everything to gain by connecting or reconnecting with people who love us. We'll create a script, we'll choose to be uncomfortable and vulnerable, and we'll choose to roll the dice. This chapter won't tickle, but it will probably be effective.

"But, Virginia," you plead, *"you don't know what I've done to my relationships!"* And you're right. However, Virginia has seen this work enough times that she had to include it here. Just walk with us for a bit.

LET'S BEGIN

Awful things happen in our personal relationships when we have PTSD. Persistent negative beliefs about ourselves, other people, and the world are like a shotgun blast to our personal relationships.

This is true even with the people who we care about, and care about us the most: a battle buddy, parent, spouse, child, or lifelong friend. We may not even realize we have PTSD when our relationships turn south.

Let's talk about the Big Ugly. We may not know we have PTSD, but we suspect something is off. We may feel like we're in a funk or not feeling like ourselves.

We know that something about us is different and not in a good or cute way.

Our loved ones know something is off, too.

They may not know exactly what is wrong, but they know something is off.

And *we know they know* something is off.

And they know we know they know something is off.

Our PTSD becomes the metaphorical elephant in the room.

This means that there is something in the room that is obvious. Everyone knows it's there, yet no one talks about it because it is too uncomfortable to do so.

Our PTSD is as obvious, distressing, and awkward as a massive elephant in a small room. We know our loved ones are worried about us, and *they know we know*. Our loved ones may not want to upset us or make us feel suicidal by talking about our symptoms. They might not know what PTSD is, or maybe they are genuinely frightened about what might happen if they upset the balance by breaking the silence. We may not bring it up because *we know* our PTSD is stressing them out. *We know* they are scared, and *we know* they don't know what to say. If we knew what to do, we would already have done it.

Rather than talk about our PTSD with the people we love the most, we choose to avoid them, and we're back to criterion C (Avoidance) rearing its ugly head.

It's easy for us to fall into avoidance. It often starts with the best of intentions. We may try to spare our loved ones from our symptoms, or we may be frightened for their safety.

We jump into a shame spiral and isolate ourselves from the people who love us and can support us the most. Maybe when we interact with others, we get angry or frustrated or lose it.

And we might start drawing conclusions that aren't true, like that they are better off without us.

Here's the stubborn thing about love.
It doesn't give up easily.

Sometimes, our loved ones reach false conclusions, too. Without information, the brain fills in the gaps to explain why things are different.

Maybe we're not cool with meeting up in public because crowds freak us out. Our friend, on the other hand, thinks we're mad at them about something.

We don't go to the school play because we don't want to have a panic attack in public. And our child thinks it's because they didn't get a big enough part.

We don't read a bedtime story to our child because we don't want to cry in front of them. Meanwhile, our child thinks, "Mommy doesn't read to me anymore because I'm a bad kid."

We know this hurts to hear, and we're saying this to you with love.

In the absence of an explanation from us, our loved ones will reach conclusions all on their own. It will probably be dead wrong, and it will probably become another, bigger, uglier, smellier, more awkward elephant in the room that we all choose not to discuss.

You may be reading this *after* the divorce was already finalized, or *after* we told someone we never wanted to speak with them again, or *after* the kids left for college.

We get that our PTSD may have already sledge-hammered our relationships, but we want to talk about how to invite those relationships back.

THE ELEVATOR SPEECH

We get the term "elevator speech" from the business world. It's brief, about 30 seconds (the time it takes to ride from the bottom to the top of a building in an elevator).

Its intent is to clearly and succinctly state our purpose.

Our Elevator speech has 7 distinct parts:

1. Ask permission to speak without interruptions and wait for a response.
2. Introduce our elephant: own our emotions/lack of emotion, and let them know we're okay.
3. Own our past. Own our narrative. Speak plainly.
4. Describe our turning point—epiphany.
5. Ask for buy-in and support. Manage Expectations.
6. Love them.
7. Silence.

1. Ask permission.

Before rolling out our elevator speech, it's important that we let our loved one know that we want to talk to them about something important, and we will need about 30 seconds of uninterrupted time to do it.

No questions, no interjections, just 30 seconds of them listening to us with an open mind.

It's important to recognize that not everyone we love will be on board for this, and that's okay.

Relationships take two people, and it is incredibly important that we choose to honor others' boundaries. Because honoring someone else's boundaries is a way we show love and respect for them as a person.

We ask for permission right off the bat. It may sound like this:

"I'm thankful that we have this time alone together because there is something important I'd like to talk to you about. If it's okay, I'd like to say it all at once and I promise it will only take about 30 seconds. Would it be okay if I got this all out at once - with no questions?"

After asking permission, wait for a verbal yes. Only after that, proceed.

Let's say our loved one is an interrupter. That's okay. If they interrupt, just ask again, "Would it be okay with you if I got this all out? I promise I will answer any questions you have in about 30 seconds."

What if they say no?

This happens, and it's okay. Let them know that if they change their mind, we are available. Reaffirm that we care about them and respect their boundaries.

It may sound something like this:

"I completely understand, and I respect your boundaries. If you change your mind, please know that I would value talking with you."

Then, leave it alone. They will talk to you when they are ready.

2. Introduce our elephant.

We believe that whenever there is an elephant in the

room, we are smart to introduce it. We will probably have a lot of uncomfortable feelings when we choose to talk to our loved one; nervous, emotional, or frustrated.

We may feel completely numb and find it hard to connect. All of that is okay. We'll name our feelings and let our loved one know that we are all right. It may sound like this.

"I have to be honest with you. I feel really nervous talking to you right now. If I sound shaky, it's because I am, but I'll be okay."

Or,

"I realize I might sound like I'm not feeling anything right now. It's hard for me to connect, but I promise you that I want to."

3. Own our past.

This is an opportunity for us to own our behavior and not make any excuses. Let's remember that this is an elevator speech, so keep it concise. We cannot stress this enough. *Keep it simple.* This is not making amends. This is not talking to our therapist. So keep it short, and stay on point. There will be time to go in depth, and the time is not during our elevator speech.

Remember, if we are taking more than 60 seconds, we are doing it wrong.

It may sound like this:

"I know that things have been off. I've been drinking too much and spending a lot of time alone."

Or,

"I've had a terrible couple of years. I've struggled with feeling down. I recognize that this has affected you, too."

Nothing we are saying is a revelation. We are simply naming another elephant in the room. We are telling our loved one that we've been struggling, and that we recognize they see it, too.

We don't have to go into it because they already know.

We must stress that this is _not_ the time to bring up anything new. Don't say,

"I've really had a hard time these past few years... which is why I'm having an affair."

Stupid hurts. Don't do that. When we've got a bomb to drop, do it with a licensed marriage and family therapist present.

4. The epiphany.

An epiphany is the "A-ha!" moment.

We learned something we didn't know before, we saw something we didn't notice before, or we realized something we hadn't fully grasped before—and because of this, everything has shifted.

To use corporate jargon, we had a "paradigm shift" and our fundamental belief system has changed. Or, for the first time, we want our fundamental belief system to change. Our Big Two has shifted.

We either believe change is possible, or we want to change, and we are ready to take that next step.

It may sound like we're being flippant here, but this is no small thing. Epiphanies come in packages large and small, but their impact is profound. What was it that made us want to change?

It may sound like this:

"I realized after my last suicide attempt that I want to live,"

5. Ask for buy-in, manage expectations.

This is when the conversation shifts to the here and now.

We need support from our loved one, and this is the time for us to ask for it. It is also the time for us to manage expectations. This journey will not be easy, but we are dedicated to trying. It may sound something like,

"I'm here and I want to change, but I also know that this won't be easy and I'll probably screw up a lot. But I believe that with your continued support, I can do this."

Or maybe,

"I've decided to get the help I need to get better. It might take a while to see the changes in me, but I promise that I will keep trying, even if I mess up at first."

Coming back from PTSD is not an overnight process, and we need to let our loved ones know that we are all-in.

6. Love them.

Not everyone is comfortable with those three little words, but this is our chance to break ranks. Yes, we have to say those words. Keep it simple.

"The most important thing I want you to know is that I love you and I'm open to answering any questions you have."

7. Silence.

This is the hardest part of the elevator speech because every part of us wants to jump to the rescue or break the awkward silence. We implore you, friend, *shut the eff up (STFU).*

Don't go in for the hug. Don't try to comfort or soothe. At this moment, we must choose to be silent.

This is our loved one's time to speak, and we absolutely must respect that.

When we choose to be silent, it gives them an opportunity to feel whatever it is they feel without interjection and without judgment. Our silence honors their experience and it invites them to share their thoughts, feelings, and emotions with us.

This is our time to be in reception mode, and yes, it feels vulnerable and frightening.

This is how we reconnect. It is an invitation for them to be with us in a radically authentic way.

Radical authenticity is scary because it means that we are evicting all the elephants and choosing to be honest, even if it's messy. In our elevator speech, we choose to be messy and honest, and in our silence, we invite our loved one to be radically authentic with us. Again, it will be hard to stay silent, but it is vital.

Our loved one may not be ready to talk with us at that moment, and that's okay. They may be angry, or emotional, or completely unfazed—and it's all okay. We have opened a door that is not easily shut. From here, we can let them know that if they change their mind, we are available, and we reaffirm that we care about them and respect their boundaries. "I completely understand, and I respect your boundaries. If you change your mind, please know that I would value talking with you." They will talk to you when they are ready. That is when the real connection or reconnection is possible.

SOME NOTES

Every elevator speech is as different as our experiences, but it is important that we **follow the outline**.

Virginia developed the elevator speech on the backs of work by Robert Rosenthal and Viktor Frankl, two greats in psychology, and this strategy has helped literally hundreds of clients reconnect with their loved ones and forge a path to recovery.

Use notes to help. Talking to our loved ones about our PTSD is a nerve-wracking experience. We encourage the use of written notes, if that helps to steady you.

Just be sure to let your loved one know you are going to use some notes to feel steady.

"But..." **I hear you saying,** *"this all sounds pretty manipulative."*

You may be right. Here's the deal, friend: there is no need to reinvent the wheel when we have good science and research available to us.

We believe that the only way this is manipulative is if our words are inauthentic.

- **Place and space.**
  It's important that we choose an appropriate time and place to speak to our loved one, if we have a choice. If we're incarcerated or in the hospital, our options are limited. But if we have more freedom, it's smart to use it. We recommend a quiet place without interruptions.
- **This is an individual conversation.**
  Maybe you have six children, including two sets of

twins. Good on you, but this is not a time to load the Brady Bunch up on the couch for a family discussion. This is a one-on-one conversation. The reason is simple. Our PTSD affects no two people the same, and it is important that we honor each individual experience. This is especially true for children; one child may be sensitive, and another may not care as much—and it's all okay.

- **You will probably cry.**
  Not a sweet, white handkerchief cry, but a big ugly cry. Be smart. Have tissue on hand so you don't snot yourself. And maybe consider laying off the mascara so you don't look like the joker when those tears roll. If you don't cry, there is nothing wrong. Feeling numb is normal with PTSD and it's okay.

- **Keep it age appropriate**.
  We need to use language our loved one can understand. Our elevator speech with a parent will differ from our elevator speech with a child.

- **Practice.**
  We encourage role-playing our elevator speech before going live. Trying it with a therapist or a trusted friend is great, and it will encourage us.
  If we don't have a social support network yet, saying our elevator speech out loud in front of a mirror will help ease anxiety and nerves.

- **Write it out.**
  Some of us have such overwhelming anxiety that the idea of talking to another person is just not in the cards for us right now. That's okay. Write your elevator speech in a letter and hand it to a loved one. It doesn't matter how we connect; it matters that we choose to connect.

SOME EXAMPLES

Here are some examples of elevator speeches to help us feel confident in formulating our own. Don't worry about screwing up. What matters is that we show up and choose to be present. Yes, we will feel vulnerable.

Yes, we will feel awkward.

Yes, we will feel afraid—but we choose to do it, anyway. Even if it goes to hell, we are choosing to be brave, and that is awesome.

EXAMPLE 1

Ask Permission.

"Honey, I'm glad we have time alone tonight because there is something important that I would like to talk about. I promise it's not bad, but it is something that I need to get out all at once if that's okay. Would it be all right with you if I took 30 seconds to get this all out at once with no questions or interruptions?"

(STOP - wait for an answer.)

Introduce Our Elephant.

"I took time to write some things down on this paper because I don't want to forget anything, and it helps me feel less nervous."

Own Our Past.

"I've had a tough couple of years, and it's affected us both. I've pushed you away, and my drinking has gotten worse."

Epiphany.

"Recently, things got really dark for me, and I've decided that I need to get help for my PTSD."

Ask For Buy-In/Manage Expectations.

"I have some ideas for getting help, and I know it will not be easy. I believe that with your support, I can start this fight."

Love Them.

"I realize that I've put you through a lot. The most important thing I want you to know is that I love you, I love us, and I will do whatever it takes to make this work."

Silence.

Seriously, do whatever it takes to be silent and let your partner speak next.

EXAMPLE 2
AGE APPROPRIATE

Ask Permission.

"Hey, buddy! I have something important I want to talk to you about, if that's okay. You're not in any trouble, don't worry. I want to talk to you a little about what I've been going through. Would that be okay?"

(STOP - wait for an answer.)

Introduce Our Elephant.

"I realize that I'm crying a little, but I'm okay. Sometimes I feel so much love for you that it fills my heart and comes out of my eyeballs, and I promise you I'm okay."

Own Our Past.

"I know that we haven't been spending as much time together as we used to, and that's my fault. I was too embarrassed to tell you, but sometimes I feel scared in crowds. Sometimes, I get really angry unexpectedly, too, and it scares me."

Epiphany.

"Even though I feel scared sometimes, I've decided that I want to be the best parent I can be, so I'm going to work on facing my fears with the help of a therapist. That's a special kind of mind doctor."

Ask For Buy-In/Manage Expectations.

"This means that I'll be going to see the doctor a lot over the next few weeks. They are going to give me lots of homework assignments. I might seem grumpy, but that doesn't mean I'm grumpy with you. If I do everything the doctor asks, I'll work through all of my grumpys. And I'm hoping you might help too, with some encouragement to keep me motivated."

Love Them.

"I imagine it feels scary to see me acting angry, and it scares me too. I imagine you feel pretty lonely when I'm in one of those cranky moods. And that is why I have to get better. You are so important to me. I need you to know that. I love you. You can talk to me about any feelings you have, and I will do my best to answer all of your questions. I want to be there for you, too."

Silence.

Be silent and let your child speak next.

EXAMPLE 3

Ask Permission.

"Mom/Dad, I'm glad we have a chance to talk, even if it's just on the phone. I know you've been worried about me, and the truth is that I've been worried about me, too. I want to tell you what I've been going through and I'll need about 30 seconds to get it all out. After that, I promise I'll answer any questions you have. Would that be okay?"

(STOP - wait for an answer.)

Introduce Our Elephant.

"It's hard for me to connect with my feelings, so while it may sound like I'm numb or like I don't feel anything, I promise you that I do and I'm okay."

Own Our Past.

"I've had a tough time with work lately. The stress and pressure were really getting to me. I stopped calling you weekly like I used to because I didn't want you to worry about me, but I realize that probably made you worry more."

Epiphany.

"I've been talking to some friends, and I've decided I want to get help."

Ask For Buy-In/Manage Expectations.

"I'll be looking into getting professional help and I could use a weekly check-in again. I realize that I'm the one who stopped calling you, and I'm sorry I did that. I really miss talking to you every week."

Love Them.

"I can't imagine what it was like for you not to hear from me, and I'm so sorry. I want you to know that I love you, and I'm so thankful you are my Mom/Dad."

Silence.

Be silent and let them speak next.

These conversations are hard, but not having social support is infinitely harder.

Also, what do we really have to lose here?

Nothing!

But we have everything to gain by connecting or reconnecting with the people who love us.

CHAPTER 13 PTSD AND WORK

In the last chapter, we discussed how to talk to those people in our lives who deserve our narratives; those who support us and love us. In this chapter, we're going to talk about folks who don't. It's likely that you work with them.

Before you get offended and write a strongly worded email, we're happy for you if you are the exception and have a workplace that feels like one big, happy family. The rest of us live in Realityville with crappy bosses, catty co-workers, and faceless HR departments.

Here's the deal: Unless we are independently wealthy, before and after we get PTSD treatment, we have to go back to work.

Like our loved ones, everyone in the office knows we need help. Unlike our loved ones, they can be judgy, passive-aggressive, small-talkity, single-minded jerks who take glee in seeing us fail.

But we digress.

Here's the Bottom-Line Up Front:

*We either control the narrative,
or the narrative controls us.*

In order to reintegrate back into the workplace after getting treatment, or get support from our workplace to go out and get treatment, we have to talk to our bosses and our colleagues about our PTSD. It's not fair, and it's none of their business. We hear you. But that's life.

This chapter is going to teach us how to control our narrative and get buy-in and support from our workplace, so we can get back to doing our job.

THERE IS A NARRATIVE, AND THERE IS AN ELEPHANT

Let's be clear: there are no secrets in the workplace. When we have issues, especially mental health issues, everybody knows about it. That's not to say that what they know is accurate, but everybody knows something is up. When we make the decision not to talk about our treatment (or need for treatment), an elephant is born.

We're going to speak plainly here: choosing to ignore our PTSD or avoid talking about it at work is not realistic. We can be ten types of brilliant, but our colleagues are thinking, "Are we really not going to talk about her being in the hospital for four weeks?" or, "Are we just going to pretend he never had a panic attack in the bathroom?"

We have to address it. It's not fair. We know.

CONTROL THE NARRATIVE

How can we talk to our bosses and our colleagues about our PTSD in a way that (1) controls the narrative, and (2) gets us buy-in and possible social support (even if only superficial) so that we can get the help we need?

We are going to create an elevator speech similar to the one from the last chapter. But, unlike talking with our loved ones, this elevator speech uses our narrative to advocate for our needs.

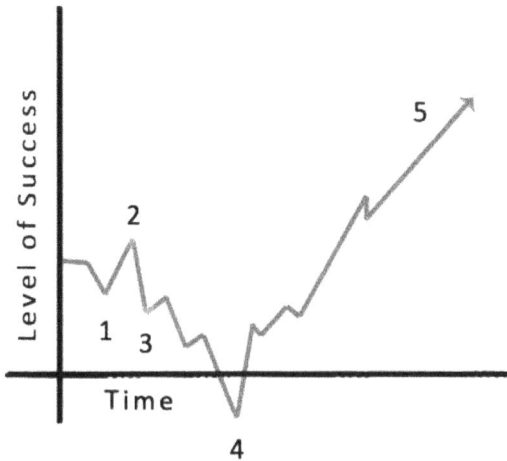

Leaning on our inspirational narrative model, this elevator speech will be tightened up and acknowledge the formality of a work setting.

Our Workplace Elevator Speech Has 6 Parts:

1. Thank them for the opportunity to talk.
2. Introduce our elephant. Own our emotions/lack of emotion.
3. Own our past. Own our narrative. Speak plainly.
4. Describe our turning point—epiphany.
5. Ask for buy-in and support. Manage expectations.
6. Thank them. Show dedication.

1. Thank them for the opportunity to talk.

When talking with HR, or anyone within our workplace chain of command, we don't always have the luxury of asking for uninterrupted time to talk. So, we'll start by thanking them for taking the time to speak with us (even if no one had a choice).

If possible, proactively ask for an opportunity to speak with the boss or HR department. This shows courage, controls the narrative, and proves how serious we are about our treatment and recovery.

2. Introduce our elephant.

We remember that whenever our elephant is in the room, we will introduce it. Again, feeling nervous, emotional, frustrated, or numb is okay. Using a note card is okay, just introduce it. It may sound like this, "In order to respect your time, I took some notes to help me stay on point," or, "It is nerve-racking to speak to you about my PTSD because of the stigma, so I thank you for your patience."

3. Own our past.

This is still an opportunity for us to own our behavior and not make any excuses. Focus on work issues and speak in concise terms. Again, no new revelations. We do not have to share details of our trauma with our bosses and colleagues; keep it simple.

4. The epiphany.

Again, this is our "A-ha!" moment when we make the choice to change. What was it that brought us to this point? This can sound like, "After the police picked me up, I realized that my life had spiraled out of control and I know I need help."

5. Ask for buy-in, manage expectations.

This is why we're here. We need support from our bosses and colleagues so we can get the help we need. It is also the time for us to manage expectations. This journey is not going to be easy, and we are dedicated to trying. It may sound something like, "I want to recover from PTSD, and I know it's not easy. I'll need to attend counseling weekly and take time off from work. I believe that with your continued support, I can do this."

Notice the word "continued" here. We are smart to use some sugar when dealing with upper management.

6. Thank them/show dedication.

Again, even if our bosses and colleagues are sub-par, it doesn't hurt to thank them.

When it comes to showing dedication, we get to be dedicated to whatever we want to be dedicated to. Just speak plainly and get to the point. "Thank you for giving me an opportunity to talk to you today. I want you to know that I'm dedicated to our team and to our mission."

We can be dedicated to finishing out a drug treatment program, or dedicated to taking good care of our family.

SOME EXAMPLES

As with the previous chapter, we want to take an opportunity to give some examples of elevator speeches to help you feel confident in formulating your own. The level of formality will depend on your workplace chain of command and/or your boss's personality.

EXAMPLE 1

Thank Them.

"Thank you for giving me the opportunity to speak to you today."

Introduce Our Elephant.

"I apologize if I sound a bit nervous. I am, and I made some notes to help me stay on point in respect of your time."

Own Our Past.

"I've been struggling lately, and it has affected my work and attendance. I tried working things out on my own and found I need more help."

Epiphany.

"I reached out to EAP and they found me professional help and resources to focus on getting better. So far it is having a positive impact."

Ask For Buy-In.

"My doctor recommended that I attend weekly appointments over the next couple months and my goal is to follow my doctor's guidance closely and get to a place where I am stronger. I would very much appreciate your support in this."

Thank Them/Show Dedication.

"Thank you for allowing me the time to speak with you today. I want you to know that I'm dedicated my work and team and I am thankful for your time and attention to my request."

EXAMPLE 2

Thank Them.

"I'd like to thank you for giving me an opportunity to address you today."

Introduce Our Elephant.

"I feel nervous talking about my mental health because I worry it might be affecting my job performance."

Own Our Past.

"In the last few months, I've had problems connecting with people at work, and I've struggled in personal ways."

Epiphany.

"The last few suicide calls I went on were really hard on me mentally, so I went to see a counselor, and I found out I have PTSD."

Ask For Buy-In.

"I realize that there's a lot of stigma about PTSD, and I'm lucky to have a team that is supportive. I believe that with your continued support, I can make a full recovery."

Thank Them/Show Dedication.

"Thank you for taking the time to hear me out. I want you to know that I'm dedicated to my work and the team, and taking care of my mental health is the best way to get back on track."

The goal of an elevator speech in the workplace is to (1) control the narrative, and (2) get buy-in and possible social support from bosses and colleagues. The first will minimize drama and the second will push us forward toward recovery. It works.

CHAPTER 14 RELAPSE PREVENTION

After we get help with our PTSD, we have to think about relapse. We tend to associate relapse with drug or alcohol use, but this simply means a period of deterioration after a period of improvement.

This can happen with PTSD, depression, anxiety, or pretty much anything relating to our health (mental or physical).

> *Relapse happens,*
> *and it's not the end of the world.*

One of the chief components of a good relapse prevention plan is to increase self-awareness and be aware of your behaviors and thoughts.

This is key because recognizing what triggers a relapse, and catching yourself in negative thoughts or behaviors, is step one in your plan to get back on track.

WHAT ARE YOUR WARNING SIGNS?

These can be things, such as the experience of certain emotions, changes in thoughts, or changes in behavior. You may run into a reminder of your trauma or get pulled into a conversation about something that reminds you of it.

Anniversaries of a traumatic event are also unavoidable and are often associated with a resurgence in PTSD symptoms.

Pay special attention to sudden changes in mood or thoughts like:

"No one cares about me or what I do. What's the point of going on?"

"I can't stand being around anyone!"

"Maybe a drink or two will take the edge off my feelings for a little while."

"I don't remember the last time I showered. I don't have the energy to do anything these days."

"Therapy is a waste of time."

Awareness of your warning signs will allow you to catch yourself and implement coping strategies you learned during treatment. Recognition is step one towards stopping these PTSD symptoms before they have a chance to become unmanageable. If you need to, this would also be a good time to check in with your therapist.

SETTING BOUNDARIES AT WORK AND IN LIFE

Strong social support fosters recovery,
but toxic relationships usher in relapse.

To manage the latter, we need to talk about boundaries.

Boundaries protect you. They let the people around you know how you define what is acceptable or unacceptable. For people who have been through traumatic experiences, however, this task is a tough one.

Experiencing trauma makes you feel unsafe and can challenge your sense of self-worth. That can lead you, and other trauma survivors, to lean back on placating or maladaptive tendencies in order to avoid conflict.

See if any of these sound familiar:

- **Can't Say "No"**

    You've had to use "Yes" to avoid conflict with a parental figure, bully, or some other figure of authority. Saying "No" has always been met with more stress, guilt, or drama than it is worth, so yes has become your default answer.

- **People Pleasing**

    You go along to get along. You've been through a nightmare and see no need to provoke anything else. At least, that's how it feels when you don't put the needs of others first. Left unchecked, this trend can get to the point where you have trouble even identifying your own needs.

- **Lack of Trust**

    A person, or people, who you've relied on for safety or protection, was the cause of your trauma, which has eroded your systems of trust. As a result, you no longer trust anyone. So why bother setting boundaries when they will just be ignored or disrespected anyway, right?

In short, to keep the peace, trauma survivors tend to not put their needs first.

That must change.

Setting healthy boundaries is an essential part of recovery. Often, trauma survivors will feel like they don't deserve to be respected or valued.

Boundaries are especially important here because the act of setting them, and holding that line, challenges the negative opinions trauma survivors have about themselves. They are an act of self-love that not only protects the survivor from others, but they also work to reinforce the survivor's reemerging sense of self-worth.

Healthy boundaries are the ultimate form of self-respect.

They say to us and the world, "I deserve to be honored, respected, and valued."

Boundaries denote confidence. Since confidence is often one of the casualties of PTSD, we have to relearn (or maybe learn for the first time) how to make a healthy, reasonable boundary, how to maintain it, and what to do if someone chooses to ignore it.

Making healthy boundaries seems like it should be easy and intuitive, but it's not.

Let's start here:

GROUND RULES

1. Healthy boundaries make healthy relationships.

There is no such thing as a healthy relationship without boundaries, whether it is a marriage relationship, a friend, colleagues, or the relationship you have with your children. Healthy boundaries say, "I deserve to be honored, respected, and valued." This is important for any healthy interpersonal relationship.

2. People do not know our boundaries unless we state them clearly and succinctly.

Yes, in a perfect world, people "should" know how to act, but suffice it to say that not everyone is great at adulting. Some people do not know that racist comments are not okay. Some people do not understand that unsolicited touching is creepy.

Let's not waste time getting mad about what "should be." Instead, let's remember that half the people we meet are below average and common sense is not common.

Boundaries are not intuitive. We must state our boundaries clearly and concisely—out loud—to other people.

3. Reasonable people respect reasonable boundaries.

The inherent problem with this is that not all people are reasonable. Sad news of the day. The world is full of psychopaths and jerks.

When people choose to ignore reasonable boundaries, they are sometimes the former and usually the latter. The problem is not our boundary, it is their *choice*.

4. Our boundaries, their choice.

We create healthy boundaries, and we have absolutely no control over other people or how they act. When we state our healthy boundaries—out loud—clearly and concisely, other people then *choose* whether they want to respect our boundaries or not.

When people choose to ignore our reasonable boundaries, they are saying in no uncertain terms, loud and clear,
"I do not respect you and I do not want a relationship with you that is not on my terms." No exceptions.

THE HOW-TO

When making a healthy boundary, we want to be sure it is reasonable, clear, and direct. We suggest using this model.

"I don't like it when you ___. Please stop."

Fill in the blank. Here are some examples:

"I don't like it when you stare. Please, stop."

"That word is offensive. Please, don't use it."

"I don't like hugging people. Can we fist bump?"

What we like about this model is that it's not attacking the person. It addresses behavior.

It's also short and to the point.

We remember that this must be a reasonable boundary.

We're not saying, *"I don't like it when you breathe, please stop,"* but we are making a legitimate, healthy boundary.

PUSH-BACK

Let's restate. Reasonable people respect reasonable boundaries. When we cross a boundary and someone lets us know, our only reasonable response is, "I'm sorry; it won't happen again." We made a mistake and now we know, going forward. It's nothing personal. End of story.

Not everyone is reasonable, and we'll probably experience push-back from time to time. This will range from a surprised, "you never said anything before," to an accusatory, "no one else seems to have a problem with it," or a full out obnoxious tantrum of, "this is who I am, and I don't have to change 'cause I don't wanna!"

Our course of action is to **simply and calmly restate our boundaries.**

Here are some examples.

"I hear you. I still find that word offensive. Please stop using it."

"It's not personal. I just don't like hugging."

"No one is trying to hurt your feelings or make you feel sad on the inside. Please, stop."

Sometimes, the push-back gets personal and downright ugly, especially if someone feels they deserve to act however they want.

Let's remember that being a jerk is their choice, and that they are choosing to say, "I don't think that you deserve to be honored, respected, or valued."

The message is loud and clear, so listen.

> *"When someone shows you who they are, believe them the first time."*
>
> Maya Angelou

IN ACTION

We swear a lot. Some people don't like it. Let's say that you are one of our students and you approach after class and say, "I don't like it when you swear. Please stop."

You know what will happen?

We'll apologize and sincerely do our best to stop swearing in front of you. We may slip up, but we will sincerely try.

The reason is simple: ***We value our relationship with our students more than the need to swear.*** We will choose to respect your boundary because we believe that everyone deserves to be honored, respected, and valued. End of story.

Not everyone values their relationships with us more than they value their need to violate perfectly reasonable boundaries.

When this happens, we can't change the person - so we may have to change the relationship.

But I Want to be Liked/Loved

Not everyone will like us, and that is okay.

Furthermore, not everyone who "should" love us chooses to act in a way that honors, values, and respects us.

When we make a boundary, others make a choice, and it is our responsibility to respect that choice - even if it means that the other person chooses to no longer be in a relationship with us.

It is tempting to get caught up in the "shoulds," as in "my parent 'should' love me," or "my spouse 'should' respect me." We urge everyone to collectively stop *should-ing* all over ourselves. Family members know how to push our buttons because they installed them.

Rejection hurts, but not as much as chasing the love of someone who has very clearly said that they choose not to honor, value, or respect us.

QUICK LIST

We've introduced a lot in this chapter, so we want to wrap it up with some quick tips for creating and maintaining healthy boundaries:

- Give ourselves permission. Everyone deserves to feel honored, respected, and valued—even us.
- Name our limits. Take time to decide for ourselves what behavior is and is not okay. If you wouldn't treat a friend that way, don't allow yourself to be treated that way.

- Practice self-awareness. If someone's behavior feels creepy or uncomfortable, this is probably a boundary.
- Be direct. We don't have to explain our reasons for having reasonable boundaries. Unreasonable people don't care anyway and are just being manipulative.
- Seek support. Social support is an important part of self-care. A therapist can be an excellent sounding board and provide good insight. So can a support group, church, and good friends.

Start small. Like any new skill, creating healthy boundaries takes practice. We can start with a small boundary that isn't too threatening and then increase to more challenging boundaries.

Learning how to create and maintain healthy boundaries will support our PTSD recovery and help us to regain confidence and self-respect.

FINAL NOTE

We wrote this book for you because we've been there before and know how to get out. Now we want you to recover, because you deserve it.

We've covered a lot: What PTSD is and isn't, Moral Injury, what treatments work, how to find treatment and social support, how to talk to others about our PTSD, and how to protect our recovery through healthy boundaries.

Our hope is that you have a lot more tools now than when you started.

Since you've stuck with us until the end, we'll leave you with this piece. Full disclosure, it is military-based, but the underlying message is one we think translates universally to those who are struggling with PTSD.

A Soldier with PTSD fell into a hole and couldn't get out. A Senior NCO went by and the Soldier with PTSD called out for help. The Senior NCO yelled, told him to suck it up, dig deep, and drive on, then threw him a shovel. But the Soldier with PTSD could not suck it up and drive on so he dug the hole deeper.

A Senior Officer went by and the Soldier with PTSD called out for help. The Senior Officer told him to use the tools his Senior NCO gave him and then threw him a bucket. But the Soldier with PTSD was using the tools his Senior NCO gave him, so he dug the hole deeper and filled the bucket.

A psychiatrist walked by. The Soldier with PTSD said, "Help! I can't get out!" The psychiatrist gave him some drugs and said, "Take this. It will relieve the pain." The Soldier with PTSD said thanks, but when the pills ran out, he was still in the hole.

A well-known psychologist rode by and heard the Soldier with PTSD crying for help. He stopped and asked, "How did you get there? Were you born there? Did your parents put you there? Tell me about yourself, it will alleviate your sense of loneliness." So, the Soldier with PTSD talked with him for an hour, then the psychologist had to leave, but he said he'd be back next week. The Soldier with PTSD thanked him, but he was still in the hole.

A priest came by. The Soldier with PTSD called for help. The priest gave him a Bible and said, "I'll say a prayer for you." He got down on his knees and prayed for the Soldier with PTSD, then he left. The Soldier with PTSD was very grateful, he read the Bible, but he was still stuck in the hole.

A recovering Soldier with PTSD happened to be passing by. The Soldier with PTSD cried out, "Hey, help me. I'm stuck in this hole!" Right away the recovering Soldier with PTSD jumped down in the hole with him. The Soldier with PTSD said, "What are you doing? Now we're both stuck here!" But the recovering Soldier with PTSD said, "Calm down. It's okay. I've been here before. I know how to get out."

-Author Unknown

ACKNOWLEDGEMENT

To our beta readers, John Lastella, Jamie Hubbard, and Dawn Matejka, as well as our anonymous contributors, this book would not be what it is today without the help you provided.

We thank you from the bottom of our hearts!

ABOUT THE AUTHOR

VIRGINIA CRUSE

Virginia Cruse is a Licensed Professional Counselor and National Certified Counselor specializing in Military Issues and Combat-Related Trauma. She provides crisis intervention and Evidence-Based Treatments for Post-Traumatic Stress Disorder, Moral Injury, Depression, Combat Operational Stress, and other diagnoses. Virginia is a certified clinician in Cognitive Processing Therapy and Prolonged Exposure Therapy and has 20+ years' experience serving Active Duty Military, Veterans, Military retirees, and family members. She is a Certified Group Psychotherapist and active American Group Psychotherapy Association member. Virginia is a former Reserve Officer, Combat Veteran, and published researcher. She has one amazing husband, Jay, and one terrible dog, Peanut.

Virginia practices in Texas, Oklahoma, Louisiana, and Arkansas. Find out more at:
https://MilitaryCounselingSA.com/

ABOUT THE AUTHOR

KATIE SALIDAS

Katie Salidas is a best-selling author of fiction and nonfiction, with more than thirty books published to date. Known for her unique genre-blending style, Salidas seamlessly bridges the gap between fantasy and reality. Since 2010 she's penned six unique Paranormal and Urban Fantasy book series. Her nonfiction offerings include, *Go Publish Yourself* and *Write (and Edit) the Damn Book*.

When she's not writing her books, Salidas is actively working to help other authors in the pursuit of publishing as a consultant, educator, and ghostwriter with Rising Sign Books.

Find out more about Katie Salidas by visiting her websites.
http://www.risingsignbooks.com/
https://www.katiesalidas.com/

Your opinion matters!

When people first look at a book, beyond the description or cover, they pay close attention to what others, like you, have to say. Reviews heavily influence that reader's decision to make a purchase.

You don't have to write a novel. That's our job!

Simply share what you thought of the book by answering two simple questions.

Was the information valuable?

Would you recommend it to someone else?

That's it!

Your opinion matters. It matters to us, because we want to ensure you are getting the most accurate and helpful information. And beyond our desire to educate you, the review you write could make (or break) the success of this book.

LINKS AND RESOURCES

HELP LINES

988 Suicide and Crisis Line
The Lifeline provides 24/7, free and confidential support for people in distress, prevention and crisis resources for you or your loved ones, and best practices for professionals in the United States.

Safe Call Now
1-206-459-3020
A 24/7 help line staffed by First Responders for First Responders and their family members. They can assist with treatment options for responders who are suffering from mental health, substance abuse and other personal issues.

Fire/EMS Helpline
1-888-731-3473
Also known as Share The Load. A program run by the National Volunteer Fire Council. They have a help line, text-based help service, and have also collected a list of many good resources for people looking for help and support.

Emergency Responder Crisis Text Line
Text BADGE to 741741

Copline (Law Enforcement Only)
1-800-267-5463
A confidential helpline for members of US law enforcement. Their website also has additional information on help and resources.

Frontline Helpline
1-866-676-7500
Run by Frontline Responder Services. Offers 24/7 coverage with
First Responder call-takers.

Kristin Brooks Hopeline
1-800-442-4673
Another national (USA) hotline for people suffering from mental
health issues.

Substance Abuse and Mental Health Services Administration
National Helpline
(800) 662-4357 or TTY – 1-800-487-4889

National Alliance on Mental Illness
1-800-950-6264

WEBSITES

Suicide.org
http://suicide.org/
List of local helplines for all 50 states. This list includes thousands
of local call numbers for every state in the US. Calling a local number can help put you in contact with nearby resources like counselors or psychiatrists faster than calling a national line.

Substance Abuse and Mental Health Services Administration
National Helpline
https://www.samhsa.gov

National Alliance on Mental Illness
https://nami.org/Home

The National Volunteer Fire Council (NVFC)
https://www.nvfc.org/
The National Volunteer Fire Council (NVFC) has a program called
"Share the Load" which provides a database of licensed mental
health professionals. Through this program, firefighters and their
families can learn about suicide and other mental health issues

through various courses, newsletters, and videos. The NVFC also offers multiple ways to access the Suicide Prevention Lifeline, including by phone, online chat, or text.

The International Association of Fire Fighters (IAFF)
https://www.iaff.org/
The International Association of Fire Fighters (IAFF) has a trained peer support network composed of fellow firefighters who understand mental health concerns and can connect members (mostly career firefighters) with community resources and mental health professionals if needed.

Behavioral Health Treatment Services Locator (USA)
https://findtreatment.samhsa.gov/
This is a government run on-line database of mental health and substance abuse treatment facilities, both inpatient and outpatient. The database is searchable by location and type of treatment needed.

EMDR Licensed Clinician Search
https://www.emdr.com/
Tool from the EMDR Institute that allows you to search for clinicians that have been trained and licensed to use EMDR. EMDR is a type of therapy that has been shown to be beneficial in treating traumatic stress and PTSD.

Anxiety and Depression Association of America (ADAA)
https://adaa.org/
Provides information on prevention, treatment, and symptoms of anxiety, depression, and related conditions

EMDR Institute
www.emdr.com

About Prolonged Exposure Therapy
https://www.med.upenn.edu/ctsa/workshops_pet.html

About Cognitive Processing Therapy
https://cptforptsd.com/

About Eye Movement Desensitization and Reprocessing
https://www.emdr.com/what-is-emdr/

ORGANIZATIONS AND SUPPORT GROUPS

Survivor's Network for Air & Surface Medical Transport
https://www.survivorsnetwork-airmedical.org/
This network provides support, education, and resources to air & surface medical organizations, personnel and their families, and works to help mitigate risk and aid in individual and organizational post-accident recovery. They also put an emphasis on sharing the stories of survivors of medical transport incidents.

Gary Sinise Foundation
https://www.garysinisefoundation.org/first-responders-outreach/
Offers grants up to $50,000 for First Responder agencies and First Responders who need assistance paying for equipment, training, medical expenses related to line-of-duty-injuries, and home modifications due to permanent disabilities.

AMR's EAP – 1-888-327-0024 or 1-888-327-1060
Employee Assistance Program for AMR employees in the US and the phone number to the 24/7 crisis/counseling line.

American Academy of Experts in Traumatic Stress
https://www.aaets.org/frontline-groups
The American Academy of Experts in Traumatic Stress, Green Cross Academy of Traumatology and CISM Perspectives' goal is to coordinate efforts to increase the support available to healthcare workers and emergency responders.

How2LoveOurCops
https://www.how2loveourcops.org/

How2LoveOurCops is a 501(c)(3) organization that is dedicated to the relational, emotional, and spiritual wellness of law enforcement families.

The Wounded Blue
https://thewoundedblue.org/services/
The Wounded Blue is working to de-stigmatize mental health within the law enforcement community through its Peer Advocate Support Program and community outreach. The Peer Advocate Support Program handles nearly 100 calls per week from officers. With each of our team members being either active duty or a former officer, many with disabling injuries, we are able to help in a way other support groups would not be able to.

The Disaster Responder Assets Network (DRAN)
https://disasterassets.org/
The Disaster Responder Assets Network (DRAN) is a volunteer non-profit (501c3) organization comprised of men and women that have dedicated their lives to the service of others. Each of us has experience as emergency and disaster responders, bringing a depth and breadth of experience that when combined creates a force far greater than the sum of its parts. We understand that the key to successfully handling any major emergency or disaster, be it natural or manmade, is to take a holistic approach.

First Responder Support Network
https://www.frsn.org/
A program dedicated to supporting the mental health and well-being of all First Responders and their families.

Next Rung
https://www.nextrung.org/
Offers free peer support via talk, text, social media messaging, email, Skype, or FaceTime. If you are in immediate need of help, please text "SUPPORT" to 1-833-NXT-RUNG (698-7864).

Hope for Emergency Responders Organization (HERO)
https://herofirst.org/
Peer Support For First Responders

NAMI Peer Support Resources
https://www.nami.org/Your-Journey/Frontline-Professionals/Public-Safety-Professionals/Peer-Support-Resources
NAMI is dedicated to improving the lives of millions of Americans affected by mental illness.

APPLICATIONS

7 Cups
https://www.7cups.com/
Website/App – Utilizes both trained listeners and licensed therapists and counselors to provide services. Trained listeners are laypeople trained in active listening who provide free confidential support. Users can also establish a relationship with a licensed professional for a fee. Not First Responder specific, but they allow you to pick your listener and therapist so you can find someone who you're likely to be able to connect with.

IntelliCare
https://intellicare.cbits.northwestern.edu/
App (Android only) – IntelliCare is a suite of apps that work together to target common causes of depression and anxiety like sleep problems, social isolation, lack of activity, and obsessive thinking. These apps are part of a nationwide research study funded by the National Institutes of Health.

PTSD Coach
https://www.ptsd.va.gov/appvid/mobile/ptsdcoach_app.asp
Website/App – Designed by the National Center for PTSD (a division of the VA). PTSD Coach provides information about diagnosing and treating PTSD, the ability to track symptoms, information on handling stress, and direct links to support and help. Canadian version in French available for iPhone.

Lighthouse Health & Wellness
https://www.lighthousehw.org/

Lighthouse Health & Wellness is an in-hand, on-demand, 100% confidential health and wellness platform available at no cost to our nation's public safety agencies.

Lighthouse was designed to provide your employees and their families anonymous access to your agency's existing health and wellness programs, along with a growing library of the latest educational health and wellness information and tools that have been tailored to the unique needs of those working in public safety.

VOCABULARY QUICK REFERENCE

We absolutely have to know our symptoms better than anyone else – this includes our doctors and/or our therapists. This book has been a heavy read, and we don't want you to have to search for the simple stuff. Use this section as a quick reference guide to help you locate the exact term you need.

Acceptance and Commitment Therapy (ACT): A form of Mindfulness-Based Cognitive Therapy that seeks to develop psychological flexibility and encourages people to embrace their thoughts and feelings rather than fighting or feeling guilty for them.

Acute Stress Disorder (ASD): Is the continuing and extreme traumatic stress response that significantly interferes with daily life in the month following the traumatic exposure.

Acute Trauma: Exposure to a single traumatic event.

Adaptive Disclosure: Prolonged Exposure Therapy is supplemented with various perspective taking interventions involving imaginal dialogues with a "moral authority" who judges, but also has the authority to forgive the person for their breach of morality or ethics.

Avoidance: The DSM defines this as avoiding internal things (like memories, thoughts, or feelings) or avoiding external things (like people, places, and things that remind us of the trauma).

Betrayal Blindness: A term used to describe an unwillingness to recognize abuse that is ongoing.

Bilateral Stimulation (BLS): Consists of alternating right and left stimulation, whether it's tapping of the toes or tapping on the shoulders. It can also include audio or visual stimulation with the use of light. This stimulation may include eye movements, taps, or tones.

Body Scan: In EMDR therapy, this is the step where the client recognizes changes in their body sensations when thinking of negative triggers. It can reveal tension points to triggers that still need to be targeted by the therapist for additional processing.

Burnout (BO): The consequences of severe stress and high ideals in "helping" professions. It is a syndrome resulting from chronic workplace stress that has not been successfully managed.

Cognitive Processing Therapy (CPT): Includes impact statements and workbook exercises used to identify and address unhelpful thinking patterns related to safety, trust, power and control, esteem, and intimacy. The therapist will ask questions and work with you to recognize unhelpful thinking patterns, reframe our thoughts, reduce our symptoms, and come to a better understanding about yourself and your relationships.

Compassion Fatigue: Refers to a set of negative psychological symptoms that caregivers experience in the course of their work while being exposed to direct traumatic events or through Secondary Trauma.

Complex PTSD (C-PTSD): The C- distinction reflects the complexity of issues that develop due to the repetitive nature of the trauma experienced over a long period of time. Often stemming from childhood, the extended duration of traumatic experiences often necessitates an altered and longer approach to treatment, emotional regulation skill building to overcome learned behaviors and habits that formed as coping mechanisms.

Chronic Trauma: Ongoing or prolonged exposure to traumatic stress or traumatic events.

Complex Trauma: Exposure to multiple forms of trauma or traumatic events.

Co-Occurring Disorders: When we are diagnosed with two or more simultaneously occurring conditions. This is unbelievably common with PTSD. For example, we'll have PTSD and a substance or alcohol abuse problem at the same time, or PTSD and depression. The most common co-occurring disorders seen with PTSD are anxiety, depression, drug/alcohol misuse, eating disorders, and OCD.

Cumulative Trauma: The toll of repeated exposure to traumatic events is what is referred to as Cumulative Trauma, and if ignored, can have devastating effects on your well-being.

Desensitization: A treatment or process that diminishes emotional responsiveness to a negative, aversive, or positive stimulus after repeated exposure to it.

Diagnostic and Statistical Manual, Version Five (DSM-5): Is a big purple book that should be on our therapist's bookshelf. Version five came out in 2013 and changed the definition of PTSD.

Dissociation: A 50-cent word that means disconnection.

Emotional Dysregulation: Describes an emotional response that is poorly regulated and does not fall within the traditionally accepted range of emotional reaction. It may also be referred to as marked fluctuation or a mood swing.

Emotional Regulation: The ability to exert control over one's own emotional state. It may involve behaviors such as rethinking a challenging situation to reduce anger or anxiety, hiding visible signs of sadness or fear, or focusing on reasons to feel happy or calm.

Evidence-Based Treatment (EBTs): Treatments that have been peer-reviewed with substantial and verifiable scientific evidence to prove they work most of the time, for most people.

Eye-Movement Desensitization and Reprocessing (EMDR): An eight-phase treatment that focuses attention on three distinct time periods: the past, present, and future while engaging in Bilateral Stimulation (BLS) to help replace the negative memory or thought with positive ones. It is believed that BLS activates both hemispheres of the brain, which can have a soothing effect by dimming the intensity of the memory while allowing the client space to process it without an overwhelming psychological response.

Gaslighting: A way of invalidating through persistent undermining, another person's reality by denying facts, the environment around them, or their feelings.

Guilt: A negative feeling related to a particular action.

Habituation: In PE Therapy, this is a decrease in response to a stimulus after repeated presentations.

Impact Statement: In CPT, this is a detailed account of your traumatic experience, including sensory details that you remember. This process of writing it out, allows exploration of the thoughts and beliefs about the trauma.

Institutional Betrayal: Wrongdoings perpetrated by an institution upon individuals who depend on that institution. This includes any failure to prevent or appropriately respond to wrongdoings perpetrated by members of, or within, the institution.

Intimidation: Creating fear by using looks, actions, gestures, a loud voice, smashing things, or destroying property.

Intrusion Symptoms: Unwanted and involuntary intrusive symptoms of PTSD that includes: distressing thoughts, images, or memories; flashbacks; disassociation; nightmares, distressing reminders of our trauma; and body cues.

Moral Distress: A form of psychological pain that arises when an individual is expected to make the right decision, but is unable to do so due to an internal or external factor.

Moral Injury: Perpetrating, failing to prevent, or bearing witness to acts that transgress deeply held moral beliefs and expectations.

Police Complex Spiral Trauma (PCST): Another term that addresses the cumulative impact of trauma experienced by LEOs over time due to the frequent exposure to traumatic events.

Post-Traumatic Stress Disorder (PTSD): The result of exposure to trauma, where the symptoms of that trauma persist or get worse in the weeks and months after the traumatic event.

Prolonged Exposure Therapy (PE): Utilizes a technique called "imaginal exposure." After learning breathing techniques to manage anxiety, we imagine and describe the traumatic event in detail with guidance from a therapist. After the imaginal exposure, we process the experience with our therapist. Sessions are recorded on audio to listen to between sessions; this helps us to further process our emotions and practice breathing techniques.

Secondary Traumatic Stress (STS): Is the stress resulting from helping or wanting to help a traumatized or suffering person.

Shame: A feeling of diminished self-worth that is not related to any particular action.

Somatic Therapy/Work: Somatic means "relating to the body." Somatic psychotherapy is an umbrella term for therapies that center on the mind-body connection.

Sub-Threshold Posttraumatic Stress Disorder (S-PTSD): The psychological, emotional, and physical distress associated with repeated exposure to traumatic events, either directly or indirectly, that can cause ongoing distress but does not meet all criteria for PTSD.

Threats: Making threats to do something to hurt a person emotionally or physically.

Toxic Positivity: A form of invalidation that falls into the family of Gaslighting (See Emotional Abuse). Instead of facing difficult emotions, Toxic Positivity rejects or ignores the negative in favor of a cheerful, often falsely positive, facade.

Traumatic Stress (TS): Is the response to a traumatic event. It is a normal reaction to a terrible event, but symptoms usually get better over time.

Treatment-Resistant PTSD (TR-PTSD): An individual who, despite adequate treatment with antidepressants and cognitive behavioral therapy, still meets the criteria for PTSD is considered treatment-resistant. Resistance to PTSD treatment can be associated with more severe cases of PTSD, the experience of multiple traumas, the type of trauma, or other co-occurring psychiatric disorders and gender-related issues.

Trigger: Memories, objects, people, etc. that spark intense negative emotions.

Vicarious Trauma: A theoretical term that focuses on the profound negative changes in a person's worldview due to the exposure to traumatic content of the people they help.

BIBLIOGRAPHY

[1] Klimley, Kristin E.; Van Hasselt, Vincent B.; Stripling, Ashley M. (November 2018). "Posttraumatic stress disorder in police, Firefighters, and emergency dispatchers". *Aggression and Violent Behavior*. **43**: 33–44. doi:10.1016/j.avb.2018.08.005. ISSN 1359-1789. S2CID 149632078.

[2] SAMHSA Disaster Technical Assistance Center Supplemental Research Bulletin First Responders: Behavioral Health Concerns, Emergency Response, and Trauma May 2018 https://www.samhsa.gov/sites/default/files/dtac/supplementalresearchbulletin-firstresponders-may2018.pdf

[3] Sean Bell, Yarin Eski, 'Break a Leg—It's all in the mind': Police Officers' Attitudes towards Colleagues with Mental Health Issues, Policing: A Journal of Policy and Practice, Volume 10, Issue 2, June 2016, Pages 95–101, https://doi.org/10.1093/police/pav041

[4] Haugen, Peter T.; McCrillis, Aileen M.; Smid, Geert E.; Nijdam, Mirjam J. (November 2017). "Mental health stigma and barriers to mental health care for First Responders: A systematic review and meta-analysis". *Journal of Psychiatric Research*. **94**: 218–229. doi:10.1016/j.jpsychires.2017.08.001. ISSN 0022-3956. PMID 28800529.

[5] Prati, Gabriele; Pietrantoni, Luca (April 2010) "The relation of perceived and received social support to mental health among First Responders: a meta-analytic review". *Journal of Community Psychology*. **38** (3): 403–417. doi:10.1002/jcop.20371. ISSN 0090-4392.

[6] Walker A, McKune A, Ferguson S, Pyne DB, Rattray B. Chronic occupational exposures can influence the rate of PTSD and depressive disorders in first responders and military personnel. Extrem Physiol Med. 2016;5:8. Published 2016 Jul 15. doi:10.1186/s13728-016-0049-x https://www.ncbi.nlm.nih.gov/pmc/articles/PMC4947320/

[7] Kristin E. Klimley, Vincent B. Van Hasselt, Ashley M. Stripling, *Posttraumatic stress disorder in police, firefighters, and emergency dispatchers*, Aggression and Violent Behavior, Volume 43, 2018, Pages 33-44, ISSN 1359-1789, https://doi.org/10.1016/j.avb.2018.08.005. https://www.sciencedirect.com/science/article/pii/S1359178918302416

[8] Leslie M. Carson, Suzanne M. Marsh, Margaret M. Brown, Katherine L. Elkins, Hope M. Tiesman, An analysis of suicides among first responders Findings from the National Violent Death Reporting System, 2015 2017, Journal of Safety Research, Volume 85, 2023, Pages 361-370, ISSN 0022-4375, https://doi.org/10.1016/j.jsr.2023.04.003

[9] Karolina Krysinska & David Lester (2010) Post-Traumatic Stress Disorder and Suicide Risk: A Systematic Review, Archives of Suicide Research, 14:1, 1-23, DOI:10.1080/13811110903478997
https://www.tandfonline.com/doi/abs/10.1080/13811110903478997

[10] Figley, Charles R. (Ed.). (1995). Compassion Fatigue: Coping with Secondary Traumatic stress disorder in those who treat the traumatized. Brunner/Mazel. https://psycnet.apa.org/record/1995-97891-000

[11] Vicarious Trauma Fact Sheet American Counseling Association
https://www.counseling.org/docs/trauma-disaster/fact-sheet-9---vicarious-trauma.pdf

[12] Transforming the Pain: A Workbook on Vicarious Traumatization (Norton Professional Books (Paperback)) by Karen W. Saakvitne and Laurie Anne Pearlman | Oct 17, 1996 https://www.amazon.com/Transforming-Pain-Vicarious-Traumatization-Professional/dp/0393702332

[13] Figley,Charles R. (Ed.). (1995). Compassion Fatigue: Coping with Secondary Traumatic stress disorder in those who treat the traumatized. Brunner/Mazel. https://psycnet.apa.org/record/1995-97891-000

[14] Mathieu, F. (2012). The Compassion Fatigue Workbook: Creative Tools for Transforming Compassion Fatigue and Vicarious Traumatization (1st ed.). Routledge. https://doi.org/10.4324/9780203803349

[15] Rajeswari, H., Sreelekha, B., Nappinai, S., Subrahmanyam, U., & Rajeswari, V. (2020). Impact of accelerated recovery program on Compassion Fatigue among nurses in South India. Iranian Journal of Nursing and Midwifery Research, 25(3), 249–253. Doi:10.4103/ijnmr.ijnmr_218_19 Retrieved from https://www.ncbi.nlm.nih.gov/pmc/articles/PMC7299415/

[16] Dumitrascu, C.I., Mannes, P., Gamble, L., Selzer, J. (2014, January). Substance Use Among Physicians and Medical Students. Retrieved from http://msrj.chm.msu.edu/wp-content/uploads/2014/04/MSRJ-Winter-2014-Substance-Use-Among-Physicians-and-Medical-Students.pdf

[17] Hawkins, H.C. (2001). Police officer Burnout: A partial replication of Maslach's Burnout inventory. Police Quarterly, 4(3), 343-360.

[18] Petrie, K., Milligan-Saville, J., Gayed, A., Deady, M., Phelps, A., Dell, L., Forbes, D., Bryant R. A., Calvo R. A., Glozier, N., Harvey, S.B. Prevalence of PTSD and common mental disorders amongst ambulance personnel: a systematic review and meta-analysis. Soc Psychiatry Epidemiol. 2018 Sep;53(9):897-909. Doi: 10.1007/s00127-018-1539-5. Epub 2018 Jun 5. PMID: 29869691.

[19] Cocker F, Joss N. Compassion Fatigue among Healthcare, Emergency and Community Service Workers: A Systematic Review. Int J Environ

Res Public Health. 2016 Jun 22;13(6):618. doi: 10.3390/ijerph13060618. PMID: 27338436; PMCID: PMC4924075. https://www.ncbi.nlm.nih.gov/pmc/articles/PMC4924075/

[20] Vicarious Trauma Fact Sheet American Counseling Association https://www.counseling.org/docs/trauma-disaster/fact-sheet-9---vicarious-trauma.pdf

[21] Transforming the Pain: A Workbook on Vicarious Traumatization (Norton Professional Books (Paperback)) by Karen W. Saakvitne and Laurie Anne Pearlman | Oct 17, 1996 https://www.amazon.com/Transforming-Pain-Vicarious-Traumatization-Professional/dp/0393702332

[22] Patricia Smith, the founder of the Compassion Fatigue Awareness project https://www.youtube.com/watch?V=7keppa8xras

[23] McLaughlin KA, Koenen KC, Friedman MJ, Ruscio AM, Karam EG, Shahly V, Stein DJ, Hill ED, Petukhova M, Alonso J, Andrade LH, Angermeyer MC, Borges G, de Girolamo G, de Graaf R, Demyttenaere K, Florescu SE, Mladenova M, Posada-Villa J, Scott KM, Takeshima T, Kessler RC. Subthreshold posttraumatic stress disorder in the world health organization world mental health surveys. Biol Psychiatry. 2015 Feb 15;77(4):375-84. doi: 10.1016/j.biopsych.2014.03.028. Epub 2014 Apr 12. PMID: 24842116; PMCID: PMC4194258. https://www.ncbi.nlm.nih.gov/pmc/articles/PMC4194258/

[24] Papazoglou K. (2013). Conceptualizing police complex spiral trauma and its applications in the police field. Traumatology 19:196 10.1177/1534765612466151 https://psycnet.apa.org/doiLanding?doi=10.1177%2F1534765612466151

[25] What is Burnout? https://www.ncbi.nlm.nih.gov/books/NBK279286/

[26] What Firefighters Want survey results https://www.firerescue1.com/mental-health/buyer-beware-a-message-from-stressed-out-firefighters

[27] ICD-11 for Mortality and Morbidity Statistics - QD85 Burnout https://icd.who.int/browse11/l-m/en#/http://id.who.int/icd/entity/129180281

[28] Kaschka, W.P., Korczak, D., & Broich, K. Burnout: a Fashionable Diagnosis https://www.ncbi.nlm.nih.gov/pmc/articles/PMC3230825/#R8

[29] Elpern EH, Covert B, Kleinpell R. Moral distress of staff nurses in a medical intensive care unit. Am J Crit Care. 2005 Nov;14(6):523-30. PMID: 16249589. https://pubmed.ncbi.nlm.nih.gov/16249589/

[30] Jameton, A. (1984). *Nursing practice: The ethical issue*s. Englewood Cliffs, NJ: Prentice-Hall.

[31] Jameton, A. (1993). Dilemmas of moral distress: Moral responsibility and nursing practice. AWHONNS Clinical Issues in Perinatal & Womens Health Nursing, 4(4), 542-551.

[32] Corley, M. C. (2002). Nurse moral distress: A proposed theory and research agenda. Nursing Ethics, 9(6), 636-650. https://journals.sagepub.com/doi/10.1191/0969733002ne557oa

[33] Ann Baile Hamric abhamric@vcu.edu , Christopher Todd Borchers & Elizabeth Gingell Epstein (2012) Development and Testing of an Instrument to Measure Moral Distress in Healthcare Professionals, AJOB Primary Research, 3:2, 1-9, DOI: 10.1080/21507716.2011.652337 https://doi.org/10.1080/21507716.2011.652337

[34] Rességuier A. The moral sense of humanitarian actors: an empirical exploration. Disasters. 2017;42:1–62. https://doi.org/10.1111/disa.12234

[35] Morley, Jeff. "Moral distress, Compassion Fatigue, and bureaucratic cruelty." Gazette 65, no. 3 (2003): 34-35. https://www.ojp.gov/ncjrs/virtual-library/abstracts/moral-distress-compassion-fatigue-and-bureaucratic-cruelty

[36] Wounds of the Spirit: Moral Injury in Firefighters February M Schimmelpfennig · 2023 https://www.ffbha.org/wp-content/uploads/2023/02/Moral-Injury-White-Paper-2-9-23.pdf

[37] Colwell, C. B. (2016). Refusal in the field. when can an uncooperative patient refuse care and transport? JEMS: A Journal of Emergency Medical Services, 41(8), 45.

[38] Elpern EH, Covert B, Kleinpell R. Moral distress of staff nurses in a medical intensive care unit. Am J Crit Care. 2005 Nov;14(6):523-30. PMID: 16249589. https://pubmed.ncbi.nlm.nih.gov/16249589/

[39] Shay, J. (2014). Moral injury. Psychoanalytic Psychology, 31(2), 182–191. https://doi.org/10.1037/a0036090

[40] Litz, B. T., Stein, N., Delaney, E., Lebowitz, L., Nash, W. P., Silva, C., et al. (2009). Moral injury and moral repair in war veterans: a preliminary model an intervention strategy. *Clin. Psychol. Rev.* 29, 695–706. doi: 10.1016/j.cpr.2009.07.003 https://www.sciencedirect.com/science/article/abs/pii/S0272735809000920?via%3Dihub

[41] Litz, B. T., Stein, N., Delaney, E., Lebowitz, L., Nash, W. P., Silva, C., et al. (2009). Moral injury and moral repair in war veterans: a preliminary model an intervention strategy. *Clin. Psychol. Rev.* 29, 695–706. doi: 10.1016/j.cpr.2009.07.003 https://www.sciencedirect.com/science/article/abs/pii/S0272735809000920?via%3Dihub

[42] Joannou, M., Besemann, M., & Kriellaars, D. (2017). Project trauma support: Addressing moral injury in first responders. Mental Health in

Family Medicine, 13, 418–422.

[43] Firefighter Behavioral Health Alliance White Paper Series No. 1
https://www.ffbha.org/wp-content/uploads/2023/02/Moral-Injury-White-Paper-2-9-23.pdf

[44] Compromised conscience: A scoping review of moral injury among firefighters, paramedics, and police officers. Frontiers in Psychology, 12, 681. https://doi.org/10.3389/fpsyg.2021.639781.

[45] Williamson, V., Stevelink, S., & Greenberg, N. (2018). Occupational moral injury and mental health: Systematic review and meta-analysis. The British Journal of Psychiatry, 212(6), 339-346. Doi:10.1192/bjp.2018.55 https://www.cambridge.org/core/services/aop-cambridge-core/content/view/5DC1F4B8FFF97DA27940940FE87CB527/s0007125018000557a.pdf/occupational-moral-injury-and-mental-health-systematic-review-and-meta-analysis.pdf

[46] Chopko B. A., Facemire V. C., Palmieri P. A., Schwartz R. C. (2016). Spirituality and health outcomes among police officers: empirical evidence supporting a paradigm shift. Crim. Just. Stud. 29, 363–377. 10.1080/1478601X.2016.1216412 https://www.tandfonline.com/doi/full/10.1080/1478601X.2016.1216412

[47] Koenig, H. G., & Al Zaben, F. (2021). Moral injury: An increasingly recognized and widespread syndrome. Journal of religion and health, 60(5), 2989-3011. https://doi.org/10.1007/s10943-021-01328-0.

[48] Joannou, M., Besemann, M., & Kriellaars, D. (2017). Project trauma support: Addressing moral injury in first responders. Mental Health in Family Medicine, 13, 418–422.

[49] Beyond PTSD: Soldiers Have Injured Souls by Diane Silver, Miller-Mccune https://truthout.org/articles/beyond-ptsd-soldiers-have-injured-souls/

[50] Moral injury and moral repair in war veterans: A preliminary model and intervention strategy. Litz, et al. https://www.sciencedirect.com/science/article/abs/pii/S0272735809000920?Via%3Dihub

[51] "Institutional Betrayal" as connected with betrayal trauma theory was introduced in presentations by Freyd in early 2008 , Platt, Barton, & Freyd (2009) , and in a 2013 research report (Smith & Freyd, 2013). Institutional betrayal is a core focus of the book *Blind to Betrayal*, by Freyd and Birrell, 2013. The current and most definitive exploration of institutional betrayal is presented in the *American Psychologist* (Smith & Freyd, 2014). Also see Platt, M., Barton, J., & Freyd, J.J. (2009). A Betrayal Trauma Perspective on Domestic Violence. https://dynamic.uoregon.edu/jjf/articles/pbf09.pdf

[52] Gómez, J., Smith, C, Gobin, R., Tang, S., & Freyd, J. 2016). Collusion, torture, and inequality: Understanding the actions of the American Psychological Association as institutional betrayal. Journal of Trauma & Dissociation, 17(5), 527–544.
https://doi.org/10.1080/15299732.2016.1214436

[53] South Park It's Called DARVO https://southpark.cc.com/video-clips/gfwbrf/south-park-it-s-called-darvo

[54] Iheduru-Anderson K. Reflections on the lived experience of working with limited personal protective equipment during the COVID-19 crisis. Nurs Inq. (2021) 28:e12382. doi: 10.1111/nin.12382 https://pubmed.ncbi.nlm.nih.gov/33010197/

[55] https://www.psychologytoday.com/us/blog/cop-doc/201806/betrayal-the-hidden-driver-ptsd-cops

[56] Firefighter Behavioral Health Alliance White Paper Series No. 1 https://www.ffbha.org/wp-content/uploads/2023/02/Moral-Injury-White-Paper-2-9-23.pdf

[57] Rességuier A. The moral sense of humanitarian actors: an empirical exploration. Disasters. 2017;42:1–62. https://doi.org/10.1111/disa.12234

[58] Uddin H, Hasan MK, Castro-Delgado R. Effects of mass casualty incidents on anxiety, depression and PTSD among doctors and nurses: a systematic review protocol. BMJ Open. 2023 Sep 11;13(9):e075478. doi: 10.1136/bmjopen-2023-075478. PMID: 37696639; PMCID: PMC10496702. https://www.ncbi.nlm.nih.gov/pmc/articles/PMC10496702/

[59] Gallagher, Sharon and McGilloway, Sinéad (2008) *Living in Critical Times: The Impact of Critical Incidents on Frontline Ambulance Personnel: A Qualitative Perspective.* International Journal of Emergency Mental Health and Human Resilience, 9 (3). pp. 215-224. ISSN 1522-4821 https://mural.maynoothuniversity.ie/9291/

[60] Kyron, M. J., Rikkers, W., LaMontagne, A., Bartlett, J., & Lawrence, D. (2022). Work-related and nonwork stressors, PTSD, and psychological distress: Prevalence and attributable burden among Australian police and emergency services employees. *Psychological Trauma: Theory, Research, Practice, and Policy, 14*(7), 1124–1133. https://doi.org/10.1037/tra0000536

[61] Uddin H, Hasan MK, Castro-Delgado R. Effects of mass casualty incidents on anxiety, depression and PTSD among doctors and nurses: a systematic review protocol. BMJ Open. 2023 Sep 11;13(9):e075478. doi: 10.1136/bmjopen-2023-075478. PMID: 37696639; PMCID: PMC10496702. https://www.ncbi.nlm.nih.gov/pmc/articles/PMC10496702/

[62] driaenssens J, de Gucht V, Maes S. The impact of traumatic events on emergency room nurses: findings from a questionnaire survey. *Int J Nurs Stud* 2012;49:1411–22. 10.1016/j.ijnurstu.2012.07.003 https://pubmed.ncbi.nlm.nih.gov/22871313/

[63] Pajonk F-G, Cransac P, Müller V, et al.. Trauma and stress-related disorders in German emergency physicians: the predictive role of personality factors. *Int J Emerg Ment Health* 2012;14:257–68. https://pubmed.ncbi.nlm.nih.gov/23980490/

[64] Somville FJ, De Gucht V, Maes S. The impact of occupational hazards and traumatic events among Belgian emergency physicians. *Scand J Trauma Resusc Emerg Med* 2016;24:59. 10.1186/s13049-016-0249-9 https://www.ncbi.nlm.nih.gov/pmc/articles/PMC4848801/

[65] Department of Homeland Security. Active Shooter How To Respond. https://www.dhs.gov/xlibrary/assets/active_shooter_booklet.pdf

[66] The IACP Law Enforcement Active Shooter Policy 2018 https://www.theiacp.org/sites/default/files/2021-07/ActiveShooter2018-UpdatedFormat%2007.16.2021_0.pdf

[67] Butner, Briar, "The Effect of Post-Traumatic Stress Disorder on First Responders Following a Disaster: A Literature Review" (2022). Capstone Experience. 191. https://digitalcommons.unmc.edu/coph_slce/191

[68] David M. Benedek, Carol S. Fullerton, Robert J. Ursano, "First Responders: Mental Health Consequences of Natural and Humanmade Disasters for Public Health and Public Safety Workers," Annual Review of Public Health 28, no. 1 (February 2007): 55–68. https://ovc.ojp.gov/sites/g/files/xyckuh226/files/media/document/imp_responder_mental_health-508.pdf

[69] Perceptual and Memory Distortions During Officer Involved Shootings Alexis Artwohl, Ph.D. https://www.aele.org/law/2008FPJUN/wb-19.pdf

[70] Psychological First Aid Field Operations Guide

https://www.ptsd.va.gov/professional/treat/type/PFA/PFA_V2.pdf

[71] Erich J. (2014, November 1). Earlier than too late: Stopping stress and suicide among emergency personnel. *EMS World*. Retrieved from https://www.emsworld.com/article/12009260/suicide-stress-and-ptsd-among-emergency-personnel

[72] Shame vs. Guilt by Brené Brown https://brene-brown.com/blog/2013/01/14/shame-v-guilt/ and

The Power of Vulnerability TED talk by Brené Brown https://www.ted.com/talks/brene_brown_the_power_of_vulnerability?language=en

[73] Listening to Shame Brené Brown TED Talk
https://www.ted.com/talks/brene_brown_listening_to_shame?Language=en

[74] Cohen S. Social relationships and health. Am Psychol. 2004 Nov;59(8):676-684. doi: 10.1037/0003-066X.59.8.676. PMID: 15554821. https://pubmed.ncbi.nlm.nih.gov/15554821/

[75] Violanti, John M.; Andrew, Michael E.; Mnatsakanova, Anna; Hartley, Tara A.; Fekedulegn, Desta; Burchfiel, Cecil M. (2015-02-27). "Correlates of hopelessness in the high suicide risk police occupation". *Police Practice and Research*. **17** (5): 408–419. doi:10.1080/15614263.2015.1015125. ISSN 1561-4263. PMC 4703117. PMID 26752981.

[76] Uchino BN. Understanding the Links Between Social Support and Physical Health: A Life-Span Perspective With Emphasis on the Separability of Perceived and Received Support. Perspect Psychol Sci. 2009 May;4(3):236-55. doi: 10.1111/j.1745-6924.2009.01122.x. PMID: 26158961. https://pubmed.ncbi.nlm.nih.gov/26158961/

[77] First Responders Initiative https://www.firstrespondersinitiative.org/

[78] Lamia MC, et al. (2009). The white knight syndrome: Rescuing yourself from the need to rescue others. Oakland, CA: New Harbinger Publications.

[79] Morley, Jeff. "Moral distress, Compassion Fatigue, and bureaucratic cruelty." Gazette 65, no. 3 (2003): 34-35. https://www.ojp.gov/ncjrs/virtual-library/abstracts/moral-distress-compassion-fatigue-and-bureaucratic-cruelty

[80] Beaton R. D., Murphy S. A. (1995). Working with people in crisis: research implications, in *Compassion Fatigue: Coping with Secondary Traumatic Stress Disorder in those Who Treat the Traumatized*, eds Figley C. R. (New York, NY: Brunner/Mazel;), 51–81. https://api.taylorfrancis.com/content/books/mono/download?identifierName=doi&identifierValue=10.4324/9780203777381&type=googlepdf

[81] Beaton R. D., Murphy S. A. (1995). Working with people in crisis: research implications, in Compassion Fatigue: Coping with Secondary Traumatic Stress Disorder in those Who Treat the Traumatized, eds Figley C. R. (New York, NY: Brunner/Mazel;), 51–81. https://api.taylorfrancis.com/content/books/mono/download?identifierName=doi&identifierValue=10.4324/9780203777381&type=googlepdf

[82] The Association Between Abusive Policing and PTSD Symptoms Among US Police Officers Jordan DeVylder, Monique Lalane, and Lisa Fedina https://www.journals.uchicago.edu/doi/full/10.1086/703356

[83] Weiss D. S., Brunet A., Best S. R., Metzler T. J., Liberman A., Pole N.,

et al.. (2010). Frequency and severity approaches to indexing exposure to trauma: the critical incident history questionnaire for police officers. *J. Trauma. Stress* 23, 734–743. 10.1002/jts.20576
https://www.ncbi.nlm.nih.gov/pmc/articles/PMC3974917/

[84] Violanti J. M., Aron F. (1995). Police stressors: variations in perception among police personnel. *J. Crim. Justice* 23, 287–294. 10.1016/0047-2352(95)00012-F https://www.sciencedirect.com/science/article/abs/pii/004723529500012F

[85] Chopko B. A., Facemire V. C., Palmieri P. A., Schwartz R. C. (2016). Spirituality and health outcomes among police officers: empirical evidence supporting a paradigm shift. Crim. Just. Stud. 29, 363–377. 10.1080/1478601X.2016.1216412
https://www.tandfonline.com/doi/full/10.1080/1478601X.2016.1216412

[86] The National Institute for Occupational Safety and Health (NIOSH) Healthcare Workers and Work Stress https://www.cdc.gov/niosh/topics/healthcare/workstress.html

[87] Recognizing and Supporting EMS Providers with Mental Health and Substance Use Disorders https://www.jems.com/spotlight/recognizing-and-supporting-ems-providers-with-mental-health-and-substance-use-disorders/

[88] Violanti, John M.; Andrew, Michael E.; Mnatsakanova, Anna; Hartley, Tara A.; Fekedulegn, Desta; Burchfiel, Cecil M. (2015-02-27). "Correlates of hopelessness in the high suicide risk police occupation". *Police Practice and Research.* **17** (5): 408–419. doi:10.1080/15614263.2015.1015125. ISSN 1561-4263. PMC 4703117. PMID 26752981.

[89] Pinto, R. J., Henriques, S. P., Jongenelen, I., Carvalho, C., and Maia, Â. C. (2015). The strongest correlates of PTSD for firefighters: number, recency, frequency, or perceived threat of traumatic events? *J. Trauma Stress* 28, 434–440. doi: 10.1002/jts.22035 https://pubmed.ncbi.nlm.nih.gov/26389531/

[90] "9 sources of firefighter stress". *FireRescue1*. Retrieved 2019-11-26.

[91] What Firefighters Want survey results https://www.firerescue1.com/mental-health/buyer-beware-a-message-from-stressed-out-firefighters

[92] "Stress takes heavy toll on firefighters, experts say". *USA TODAY*. Retrieved 2018-09-11.

[93] Lindahl, Björn. "Why are suicide rates higher for farmers and firefighters than for librarians?". *Nordic Labour Journal*.

[94] "Special report: Firefighter behavioral health - NFPA Journal". *www.nfpa.org*. Retrieved 2018-09-11.

[95] Jahnke SA, Poston WSC, Haddock CK, & Murphy B (2016). Firefighting and mental health: Experiences of repeated exposure to trauma. *Work*, 53(4), 737–744. https://pubmed.ncbi.nlm.nih.gov/26890595/

[96] Klimley, Kristin E.; Van Hasselt, Vincent B.; Stripling, Ashley M. (November 2018). "Posttraumatic stress disorder in police, Firefighters, and emergency dispatchers". *Aggression and Violent Behavior*. **43**: 33–44. doi:10.1016/j.avb.2018.08.005. ISSN 1359-1789. S2CID 149632078.

[97] Cheryl Regehr Cheryl.regehr@utoronto.ca (2009) Social support as a mediator of psychological distress in Firefighters, The Irish Journal of Psychology, 30:1-2, 87-98, DOI: 10.1080/03033910.2009.10446300

[98] The National Institute for Occupational Safety and Health (NIOSH) Healthcare Workers and Work Stress https://www.cdc.gov/niosh/topics/healthcare/workstress.html

[99] Recognizing and Supporting EMS Providers with Mental Health and Substance Use Disorders https://www.jems.com/spotlight/recognizing-and-supporting-ems-providers-with-mental-health-and-substance-use-disorders/

[100] Violanti, John M.; Andrew, Michael E.; Mnatsakanova, Anna; Hartley, Tara A.; Fekedulegn, Desta; Burchfiel, Cecil M. (2015-02-27). "Correlates of hopelessness in the high suicide risk police occupation". *Police Practice and Research*. **17** (5): 408–419. doi:10.1080/15614263.2015.1015125. ISSN 1561-4263. PMC 4703117. PMID 26752981.

[101] Evarts B, & Stein G (2020). *US fire department profile* Retrieved from https://www.nfpa.org/News-and-Research/Data-research-and-tools/Emergency-Responders/US-fire-department-profile

[102] International Association of Fire Chiefs. (2006). *Managing Volunteer Firefighters for FLSA Compliance: A Guide for Fire Chiefs and Community Leaders* Retrieved from https://www.iafc.org/docs/default-source/1VCOS/flsamanual_small.pdf

[103] Josie Milligan-Saville, Isabella Choi, Mark Deady, Paul Scott, Leona Tan, Rafael A. Calvo, Richard A. Bryant, Nicholas Glozier, Samuel B. Harvey, *The impact of trauma exposure on the development of PTSD and psychological distress in a volunteer fire service,* Psychiatry Research, Volume 270,2018, Pages 1110-1115, ISSN 0165-1781, https://doi.org/10.1016/j.psychres.2018.06.058. https://www.sciencedirect.com/science/article/pii/S0165178117322928

[104] Stanley IH, Boffa JW, Hom MA, Kimbrel NA, & Joiner TE (2017). Differences in psychiatric symptoms and barriers to mental health care between volunteer and career firefighters. *Psychiatry Research*, 247, 236–242. https://pubmed.ncbi.nlm.nih.gov/27930964/

[105] Sean Cowlishaw, Dr Lynette Evans & Jim McLennan (2010) Balance between volunteer work and family roles: Testing a theoretical model of work–family conflict in the volunteer emergency services, Australian Journal of Psychology, 62:3, 169-178, DOI: 10.1080/00049530903510765 https://www.tandfonline.com/doi/pdf/10.1080/00049530903510765

[106] The National Volunteer Fire Council (NVFC) https://www.nvfc.org/

[107] The International Association of Fire Fighters (IAFF) https://www.iaff.org/

[108] Stanley IH, Boffa JW, Hom MA, Kimbrel NA, & Joiner TE (2017). Differences in psychiatric symptoms and barriers to mental health care between volunteer and career firefighters. *Psychiatry Research*, 247, 236–242. https://pubmed.ncbi.nlm.nih.gov/27930964/

[109] Sean Cowlishaw, Dr Lynette Evans & Jim McLennan (2010) Balance between volunteer work and family roles: Testing a theoretical model of work–family conflict in the volunteer emergency services, Australian Journal of Psychology, 62:3, 169-178, DOI: 10.1080/00049530903510765 https://www.tandfonline.com/doi/pdf/10.1080/00049530903510765

[110] Backcountry Search and Rescue Study https://cpw.state.co.us/Documents/About/BSAR/Backcountry-Search-and-Rescue-Study.pdf

[111] A Cross-Sectional Analysis of Traumatic Stress and Burnout Symptoms in Search and Rescue Volunteers https://www.jems.com/operations/traumatic-stress-and-Burnout-symptoms-in-search-and-rescue-volunteers/

[112] Al Lulla M, MS; LinLin Tian, MD, PhD; Hawnwan Philip Moy, MD; Kristen Mueller, MD; and Bridgette Svancarek, MD. CE Article: The EMS Suicide Threat2020 February 2020. Available from: https://www.hmpgloballearningnetwork.com/site/emsworld/1223779/ce-article-ems-suicide-threat

[113] Klimley, Kristin E.; Van Hasselt, Vincent B.; Stripling, Ashley M. (November 2018). "Posttraumatic stress disorder in police, Firefighters, and emergency dispatchers". *Aggression and Violent Behavior*. **43**: 33–44. doi:10.1016/j.avb.2018.08.005. ISSN 1359-1789. S2CID 149632078.

[114] Al Lulla M, MS; LinLin Tian, MD, PhD; Hawnwan Philip Moy, MD; Kristen Mueller, MD; and Bridgette Svancarek, MD. CE Article: The

EMS Suicide Threat2020 February 2020. Available from: https://www.hmpgloballearningnetwork.com/site/emsworld/12237 79/ce-article-ems-suicide-threat.

[115] Bentley MA, Crawford JM, Wilkins JR, et al. An assessment of depression, anxiety, and stress among nationally certified EMS professionals. *Prehosp Emerg Care.* 2013;17(3):330-338.

[116] Burnout Among EMS Professionals: Incidence, Assessment and Management https://www.jems.com/exclusives/Burnout-among-ems-professionals-incidence-assessment-and-management/

[117] Neale, A. V. (1991). Work stress in emergency medical technicians. Journal of Occupational Medicine. : Official Publication of the Industrial Medical Association, 33(9), 991. Retrieved from http://www.ncbi.nlm.nih.gov/pubmed/1744749

[118] Carbyne, the global leader in cloud-native emergency call management, in partnership with NENA: The 9-1-1 Association, today announced the groundbreaking findings of the inaugural Pulse of 9-1-1 State of the Industry Survey. https://cdn.ymaws.com/www.nena.org/resource/resmgr/docs/2023_Carbyne_and_NENA_The_Pu.pdf

[119] Pew study https://www.pewtrusts.org/-/media/assets/2021/11/911-call-centers-lack-resources-to-handle-behavioral-health-crises.pdf

[120] Adams, J. G., Arnold, R., Siminoff, L., & Wolfson, A. B. (1992). Ethical conflicts in the prehospital setting doi://doi-org.proxy1.library.jhu.edu/10.1016/S0196- 0644(05)81759-7

[121] Colwell, C. B. (2016). Refusal in the field. when can an uncooperative patient refuse care and transport? JEMS: A Journal of Emergency Medical Services, 41(8), 45.

[122] Rushton, C. H., Batcheller, J., Schroeder, K., & Donohue, P. (2015). Burnout and resilience among nurses practicing in high-intensity settings. American Journal of Critical Care : An Official Publication, American Association of Critical-Care Nurses, 24(5), 412-420. doi:10.4037/ajcc2015291

[123] Oh, Y., & Gastmans, C. (2015). Moral distress experienced by nurses. Nursing Ethics, 22(1), 15-31. doi:10.1177/0969733013502803

[124] Rushton, C. H. (2006). Defining and addressing moral distress: Tools for critical care nursing leaders. AACN Advanced Critical Care, 17(2), 161-168. 10.1097/00044067-200604000-00011 Retrieved from http://www.ncbi.nlm.nih.gov/pubmed/16767017

[125] GUIDE TO BUILDING AN Effective EMS Wellness and Resilience Program NAEMT. (2019). NAEMT resilience guide

https://www.naemt.org/docs/default-source/ems-preparedness/naemt-re-silience-guide-01-15-2019-final.pdf?Status=Temp&sfvrsn=d1edc892_2

[126] Recognizing and Supporting EMS Providers with Mental Health and Substance Use Disorders https://www.jems.com/spotlight/recognizing-and-supporting-ems-providers-with-mental-health-and-substance-use-disorders/

[127] 6B41-Complex post-traumatic stress disorder https://icd.who.int/browse11/l-m/en#/http://id.who.int/icd/entity/585833559

[128] Emotional Flashback Management in the Treatment of Complex PTSD https://www.psychotherapy.net/article/complex-ptsd

[129] The National Institute for Occupational Safety and Health (NIOSH) Healthcare Workers and Work Stress https://www.cdc.gov/niosh/topics/healthcare/workstress.html

[130] Haugen P. T., Evces M., Weiss D. S. (2012). Treating posttraumatic stress disorder in first responders: A systematic review. Clinical Psychology Review, 32, 370-380. https://pubmed.ncbi.nlm.nih.gov/22561967/

[131] Erich J. (2014, November 1). Earlier than too late: Stopping stress and suicide among emergency personnel. *EMS World*. Retrieved from https://www.emsworld.com/article/12009260/suicide-stress-and-ptsd-among-emergency-personnel

[132] Sean Bell, Yarin Eski, 'Break a Leg—It's all in the mind': Police Officers' Attitudes towards Colleagues with Mental Health Issues, Policing: A Journal of Policy and Practice, Volume 10, Issue 2, June 2016, Pages 95–101, https://doi.org/10.1093/police/pav041

[133] Stigma, Pluralistic Ignorance, and Attitudes Toward Seeking Mental Health Services Among Police Officers November 2015 Criminal Justice and Behavior 43(6) DOI:10.1177/0093854815613103

[134] Haugen, Peter T.; McCrillis, Aileen M.; Smid, Geert E.; Nijdam, Mirjam J. (November 2017). "Mental health stigma and barriers to mental health care for First Responders: A systematic review and meta-analysis". *Journal of Psychiatric Research*. 94: 218–229. doi:10.1016/j.jpsychires.2017.08.001. ISSN 0022-3956. PMID 28800529.

[135] Differences in psychiatric symptoms and barriers to mental health care between volunteer and career firefighters. Stanley, Boffa, Hom, Kimbrel, & Joiner, 2017 PMID: 27930964 DOI: 10.1016/j.psychres.2016.11.037 https://pubmed.ncbi.nlm.nih.gov/27930964/

[136] Police suicide in small departments: a comparative analysis. Violanti, Hartley, Mnatsakanova, Andrew, & Burchflel, 2012 PMID: 23894796 PMCID: PMC4536806 https://pubmed.ncbi.nlm.nih.gov/23894796/

[137] https://blogs.cdc.gov/niosh-science-blog/2021/04/06/suicides-first-responders/

[138] National Fallen Firefighters Foundation. (2015). Everyone goes home, 16 firefighter life safety initiatives. Retrieved from www.everyonegoeshome.com/16-initiatives/

[139] National Volunteer Fire Council. (2008). Suicide in the fire and emergency services: Adopting a proactive approach to behavioral health awareness and suicide prevention. Greenbelt, MD: Author. Retrieved from https://www.nvfc.org/wp-content/uploads/2015/09/ff_suicide_report.pdf

[140] Leslie M. Carson, Suzanne M. Marsh, Margaret M. Brown, Katherine L. Elkins, Hope M. Tiesman, An analysis of suicides among first responders â"€ Findings from the National Violent Death Reporting System, 2015â€"2017, Journal of Safety Research, Volume 85, 2023, Pages 361-370, ISSN 0022-4375, https://doi.org/10.1016/j.jsr.2023.04.003. https://www.sciencedirect.com/science/article/pii/S0022437523000415

[141] Stanley IH, Boffa JW, Hom MA, Kimbrel NA, & Joiner TE (2017). Differences in psychiatric symptoms and barriers to mental health care between volunteer and career firefighters. *Psychiatry Research*, 247, 236–242. https://pubmed.ncbi.nlm.nih.gov/27930964/

[142] Violanti, John M.; Andrew, Michael E.; Mnatsakanova, Anna; Hartley, Tara A.; Fekedulegn, Desta; Burchfiel, Cecil M. (2015-02-27). "Correlates of hopelessness in the high suicide risk police occupation". *Police Practice and Research*. 17 (5): 408–419. doi:10.1080/15614263.2015.1015125. ISSN 1561-4263. PMC 4703117. PMID 26752981.

[143] Suicide: The Forever Decision by Paul G. Quinnett https://qprinstitute.com/pdfs/Forever_Decision.pdf

[144] Advice on finding a therapist. Https://www.psychologytoday.com/us/blog/freudian-sip/201102/how-find-the-best-therapist-you

[145] APA's ethical principles of psychologists and code of conduct. https://www.apa.org/ethics/code/

[146] Certified Group Psychotherapist resource http://member.agpa.org/imis/agpa/cgpdirectory/cgpdirectory.aspx

[147] The State Of Mental Health In America https://www.mhanational.org/issues/state-mental-health-america

[148] Cohen S. Social relationships and health. Am Psychol. 2004 Nov;59(8):676-684. doi: 10.1037/0003-066X.59.8.676. PMID: 15554821. https://pubmed.ncbi.nlm.nih.gov/15554821/

[149] Otsuka T, Tomata Y, Zhang S, Tanji F, Sugawara Y, Tsuji I. The association between emotional and instrumental social support and risk of suicide death: A population-based cohort study. J Psychiatr Res. 2019 Jul;114:141-146. doi: 10.1016/j.jpsychires.2019.04.012. Epub 2019 Apr 20. PMID: 31077948. https://pubmed.ncbi.nlm.nih.gov/31077948/

[150] Uchino BN. Understanding the Links Between Social Support and Physical Health: A Life-Span Perspective With Emphasis on the Separability of Perceived and Received Support. Perspect Psychol Sci. 2009 May;4(3):236-55. doi: 10.1111/j.1745-6924.2009.01122.x. PMID: 26158961. https://pubmed.ncbi.nlm.nih.gov/26158961/

[151] Robert Rosenthal teacher experiment https://www.npr.org/sections/health-shots/2012/09/18/161159263/teachers-expectations-can-influence-how-students-perform

[152] Logotherapy https://viktorfranklamerica.com/what-is-logotherapy/

[153] Narrative therapy https://www.simplypsychology.org/narrative-therapy.html

www.ingramcontent.com/pod-product-compliance
Lightning Source LLC
Chambersburg PA
CBHW072128270326
41931CB00010B/1699